BEFORE YOU GO

FORTY DAYS OF PREPARATION FOR A SHORT TERM MISSION

A Daily Devotional

Jack Hempfling

Foreword by Peter Warren, Director of YWAM Denver

Before You Go
Forty Days Of Preparation For A Short Term Mission
by Jack Hempfling

Printed in the United States of America

ISBN 978-1-60791-351-1

www.xulonpress.com

DEDICATION

To Sandy, in honor of your heart that says "Lord, wherever You send us we'll go, and whatever You want us to do, we'll do!" It's a blessing to walk to those "wherever" places with you by my side.

ENDORSEMENTS

"**P**astor Jack Hempfling's devotional, 'Before You Go' is wonderfully done, thoughtfully constructed and full of realistic insight that challenges both missionaries preparing to go into cross-cultural ministry, as well as those already on the field. I would highly recommend that every missionary candidate prayerfully use this devotional tool, and by so doing, avoid many difficulties, and increase their fruitfulness and effectiveness once on the field. It is a great way to spiritually prepare for the work of the Lord that awaits."
Tom Brazell, Director of International Ministries, Elim Fellowship, Lima NY
www.elimfellowship.org

Over the years Harvest Preparation International Ministries has sent thousands of short term missionaries into other countries.

Our experience has taught us that the preparation of the team, and each individual on the team, has been the most important aspect of a successful short term mission. "Before You Go…Forty Days of Preparation for a Short Term Mission, a Daily Devotional," is important reading, necessary for the preparation of every seriously committed short term missionary. The mission experiences Jack shares in "Before You Go" thrill my heart! Each day's devotional just keeps getting better. I believe they will be of such benefit to anyone planning a short term mission trip. You, the reader, will be challenged, shaped, and encouraged as you embrace God's call to be His short term missionary. Thank you Jack, for giving to us this indispensable tool, "Before You Go".

Don Richter, Director
Harvest Preparation International Ministries
www.harvestpreparation.com

"Before You Go" is absolutely a vital and necessary tool for every missions pastor, short term team leader, team member or even the long term missionary. Finally we have at our fingertips, a specific strategy for the preparation of a team whose desire it is to maximize every bit of time, money and energy for the purpose of producing plenteous and lasting fruit. I have personally worked with Jack Hempfling many

times on the mission field, and know first hand his passion for the nations. The years of experience that he brings to this book more than qualify him to write this manual with authority. I am so convinced of its importance, that I will require every future team member to purchase and read "Before You GO," before we go!!!

Carol Missik, Pastor
Living Word Church, and Director,
Operation Capital City
www.occ-thenations.org

CONTENTS

ACKNOWLEDGEMENTS

M ANY THANKS TO: …
…The Redeemer's Church of Columbus,
Ohio for believing in us and for sending unlikely
short term missionary candidates like us with
your blessing. Those were our first steps into the
nations with the gospel.

…Peter Warren, Director of YWAM, Denver.
In 1985, when the Lord surprised us with the
personal command to join you, we didn't have
the money to do a Discipleship Training School.
Before we ever told you what the Lord was
saying to us back home in Ohio, you called
from Colorado to say "God wants you here; …
never mind the money issue; we'll believe with
you." We experienced His faithfulness as young
Christians, in a way like never before. Where
would we be, if you hadn't opened the door?

…Elim Bible Institute. There is no place like
you: a school with missions in its DNA, a place

to grow in the ability to hear God's voice, and the place where God built a skeleton of Biblical truth into the frame of my life.

…Elim Fellowship, whose logo reads "A Worldwide Revival Fellowship," for embracing me as a minister of the gospel. You are all three of those things: <u>worldwide</u> in vision and reach, with <u>revival</u> passion stirring in your bones, and a <u>fellowship</u> of strength for pastors and missionaries alike.

…Pastor Eric Scott, for the leadership training you gave me as your assistant at Elim Gospel Church, salted with a passion for the nations. My years under you were a gift.

…Pastor Don Richter, Director of Harvest Preparation International, for the honor of relating to you as a son to a father, and for the joy of experiencing your care, encouragement, and oversight. Thanks too for the opportunity to partner with so many churches in the Great Commission.

… Kim Leach, for your tireless editing, just the gift this book needed.

… to the many others who provided support, input, ideas, encouragement and finishing touches.

For all of your parts in this adventure, I am so grateful!

FOREWORD

By Peter Warren, Director of Youth With a Mission (YWAM), Denver

Short Term Missions is still important. Jesus said "go into all the world" almost two thousand years ago but that mandate is as relevant today as at any other time in history. In fact, we have more tools to aid in this task than any other generation that has come before us.

For example, fifty years ago the first commercial jetliner was introduced to the world, and ever since that point in time it's been possible to fly to any place on earth in about 48 hours. That's remarkable. We are now living in a global village. The whole world is at our fingertips.

Another tool at our disposal is our resources. I have a friend in South America who told me it would take him at least half a year's salary just to buy a ticket to go overseas. We don't have that problem. Most of us can save a little money here or there to go on a mission trip. For example, if you were to put aside just $25 a week, and by the way, that's about the price of going out for dinner, in one year you'd have the airfare to fly to most places on earth.

We also have the training to do this effectively. You might not think you are well equipped to represent Jesus among the nations but I beg to differ. It's not about knowledge anyway. The most powerful tool you have is your testimony, your personal relationship with Jesus Christ shared through the medium of music, dramas or practical work projects. You'll be amazed at how God uses you.

Oh, and by the way, something happens to you when you go overseas. If you haven't done this before, you might not know what I'm talking about, but there's a mantle of boldness and authority that comes over me every time I go. It's like Jesus said, "and you will receive power when the Holy Spirit has come upon you and you'll be my witnesses..." (Acts 1:8).

I've been involved in short term missions for over thirty years and have had the privilege of traveling personally to over a hundred countries.

Unfortunately I learned some things the hard way. I wish someone had given me a copy of Jack's book when I was first starting out. The manner in which he combines a down-to-earth practical wisdom with simplicity and humor is exactly what the doctor ordered. This book has incredible depth and will provoke you to stop after each reading and go deeper with God. Take 40 days and read one devotional a day leading up to the day you drive to the airport to fly out. Success doesn't just happen; it's preceded by careful preparation. This book is a way you can prepare yourself for success, and the amazing thing is it'll only take ten to twenty minutes of your time at each sitting.

Thanks, Jack, for taking the time to compile this wealth of wisdom so others can be more effective in fulfilling the great commission.

INTRODUCTION

Preparation for a short term mission is so much more than packing a toothbrush, getting your passport, practicing some dramas, and buying overseas traveler's insurance.

Preparation for a short term mission involves three things:

1) Preparation of the body

Get ready by eating right, getting in shape, learning about and preparing for the physical challenges that may await (Heat? Humid or arid? Immunizations? Medicines? Clean water? Altitude? Bugs? Exertion required?).

2) Preparation of the mind

People going on a mission trip are keenly interested in having as much information as possible. They are deeply interested in what the trip will be like, and every piece of practical information that's missing will be an opportunity for their minds to fill up with wild speculations about remote possibilities.

Will you be preparing to teach and preach? Can you discover and learn a few words and phrases of the language? What tools and equipment will you be using or need to bring? What differences in culture can you find out about before you go? Are you ready, if asked, to give a personal testimony, brief and succinct? Will you and your team be practicing drama or songs, or planning for street evangelism or a Vacation Bible School? What do we pack? Where will we stay? What about the food arrangements? These are some of the many questions that need to be answered and the plans to be made, all necessary parts of this mission experience. Finding these answers involves a lot of work on either the part of the coordinator, or leader, or the people to whom they designate.

But why does it seem that we never have enough information?

No matter how much homework is done to answer the questions of your mind in regard to your upcoming trip, something in your heart will still want to know more! The fact that you are going to unfamiliar territory, and taking a risk for God, can result in your soul being "rattled" a little by the speculation and unknown.

That's one of the reasons that it is so important to give highest priority to the third area of preparation. Prepare the heart, and the mind will find peace, and the rest of you will get in line for a great short term mission experience.

3) Preparation of the heart

While preparation of the body and mind are necessary, there is nothing that will affect the success of a short term mission team more than the level to which each member is prepared in heart! You can have the most dynamic preaching abilities, music, program, drama, and language skills, or be expert builders, and go to all the trouble of this mission trip, and yet leave hardly a trace of a mark that you were there. A team that is prepared in heart, on the other hand, may not have the most dynamic preachers on the team, but will knit with the culture, hit the bulls-eye, and leave an eternal impact. It is imperative that you take opportunity to draw close to Christ in the days preceding your mission trip. It is HIS strength, anointing, and power that you and your team need in order to leave anything of eternal value.

Open Your Heart

Sure, your life still goes on before the mission trip: responsibilities at work or school, getting the kids where they need to be, PLUS now the extra time being spent getting ready for this trip with team meetings, support raising, gathering belongings, buying necessary "stuff," completing all the paperwork. With all of that activity, who has time to ADD more prayer time?

Actually, the opposite is true! Because God Himself has called you to go on this trip, you will find yourself startled with unexpected times when the house is quiet and you're home alone. God Himself will make time for you to come away with Him if you are sensitive to Him. Maybe dinner isn't ready for another 15 minutes and you can't really start another project, or your lunch partner cancelled and you have nobody to spend that hour with. Perhaps everyone else in the house is asleep and for some reason you aren't tired.

Watch with anticipation for those windows of opportunity and do your part to spend time with the Lord. Get off the internet, turn off the TV, tune out the MP3, and leave the newspaper untouched on the counter.

Scoot into a quiet room, open God's book, get on your knees, add some fasting to your regiment of spiritual disciplines, and open your heart to the Lord. Listen to the heart of Him who said "Whom shall We send, and who will go up for Us?" to which you have replied "Here am I, Lord, send me!"

TO GET THE MOST OUT OF YOUR DEVOTIONALS

Each member of your short term mission team needs to have a copy of these devotionals for their individual use.

The devotionals are intended as a help to you as you pray with focus and effectiveness, preparing your heart for a trip into the nations. Though certainly not intended as your only source of spiritual nourishment, the devotionals will help you target important issues to address before your awesome short term mission.

Just as forty days were important to Jesus in preparing Himself for His ministry, these forty days prior to your mission trip are vital in preparing you for the unexpected and unfamiliar challenges and adventures awaiting you on the mission field.

These devotionals will be too late for those of you who wait to read them until you leave for your mission trip.

After you have used them for your "40 Days of Preparation" I encourage you to bring the book along and keep these devotionals before you throughout the journey. Team leaders may consider using these devotionals as starters for morning group devotionals while on the trip, but only AFTER the team has gone through them prior to the trip.

Every ten days you'll find an extra, supplemental feature that you can use for a special day of focused prayer. You may use it on that day, or on a different day that better suits your schedule for fasting and more prayer.

One of these supplemental prayer guides covers your team, another covers the trip logistics, and the last covers your team's ministry. Use those times to unload your concerns about the mission to the Lord, and let Him do the carrying of every worry and need.

God bless you as you prepare your heart for the awesome privilege of "going into all the world."

DAY 1
KEEPING YOUR ARROW SHARP

Ephesians 4:1-3 *I, therefore, the prisoner of the Lord, beseech you to walk worthy of the calling with which you were called, with all lowliness and gentleness, with longsuffering, bearing with one another in love, endeavoring to keep the unity of the Spirit in the bond of peace.*

Ephesians 5:3-5 *But fornication and all uncleanness or covetousness, let it not even be named among you, as is fitting for saints; neither filthiness, nor foolish talking, nor coarse jesting, which are not fitting, but rather giving of thanks. For this you know, that no fornicator, unclean person, nor covetous man, who is an idolater, has any inheritance in the kingdom of Christ and God*

It's a fascinating observation: some short term mission teams are technically very sharp, but seem to make little long term impact. Perhaps they have some incredible evangelistic drama prepared, or maybe the musical skills are excellent, or the construction challenges are met by a team that really knows what they are doing, or the preachers on the team have a lot of experience. But it's like hitting a target with a dull arrow; it just seems to bounce off and fall to the ground. What mission team wants to go through all the motions and bounce off their receiving nation like a dull arrow? Surely if you are going to carry the light of God into a dark place, you expect to penetrate that darkness!

Another team might be less skilled technically, their drama is not as polished, or they haven't as much skill …but they leave a mark on the lives of the people they ministered to with their short term mission trip. How can this be?

The answer to that question is that your long term impact depends more deeply on the team's heart preparation than it does the technical preparation. Technical preparation and excellence are important; after all, we serve an excellent God and a team should strive for excellence in practical preparation. Most importantly, however, team members must prepare their hearts to stay focused, unified, positive, pure, humble, submissive, and full of praise and faith. Combining both the practical excellence with focused heart preparation is best of all. The team doing so will be like an arrow of light that penetrates the darkness and touches people's lives.

Some heart-related issues that "dull" the arrow of any short term mission team? Pride, rebellion against the team or host leaders, division and strife among the team members, complaining about circumstances, negative attitudes, coarse language, inappropriate relationships, and impurity, are just a few. Any of these are like grinding the edge of an arrow against a hard rock. Be vigilant to keep them away from your heart.

Prayer: Father, You have an inheritance in the nations for our team and for me, and I don't want to miss this eternal inheritance due to some fleshly carelessness. Help us to stay sharp as a people of God, walking in the light, and preserving the unity You have given us, resisting the devil and every temptation of the flesh. May the "point of our ministry arrow" hit the target You are aiming us towards, and may the impact of Your Spirit strike deep into the hearts of the people. To the name of Jesus Christ be all the glory.

DAY 2
EXPECT THE UNEXPECTED

Psalm 37:23 *"The steps of the righteous are ordered by the Lord."*

It's amazing how the decision to answer God's call to a short term mission seems to set in motion opportunities for "divine appointments." Like the rudder of a ship that is effective as long as the ship is moving, the Holy Spirit's guidance and direction becomes more intense as you begin to move towards new involvement in the Lord's harvest.

Surprise opportunities can arise for you individually, and for the mission team as a group.

Even as you make preparation or raise support, a co-worker might begin asking questions in a way that creates a chance for you to share your faith. While you are excited to travel with your group on your way to a far off place, God may sit you on the plane near the lonely or hurting one to whom you can say "God cares about what you're going through." Or perhaps amid the crowded airport you'll find yourself next to someone who asks where you are headed and why. Be alert for every opportunity, for as you have now begun "moving," the Holy Spirit can set up some exciting divine appointments.

As for the plans being made for your team on the mission field, give God space to direct those plans in unexpected ways as well. It's important to work hard at preparing a ministry plan and having as much ready as possible; that level of diligence and commitment to excellence honors the Lord. Yet God may intervene in the plan and adjust the direction as you go. A surprise natural disaster can propel a team that prepared for one type of ministry to give their efforts to disaster relief instead. One team I was on left home planning to help with earthquake disaster relief, but also prepared an anointed evangelistic drama for whenever the opportunity made itself available. Once on the trip, we were asked to do that drama over and over again in the public squares and by local churches, leading many to the Lord. Though willing, we never lifted an ounce of rubble.

Daily you must be flexible as well. When thunderstorms wreaked havoc on one team's plan to conduct an evangelism campaign in the park where they expected huge crowds, the team scampered to a shelter house for cover. Some members were disappointed. The hosting national pastor, however, addressed the group: "This is a small building with not much space, but we have a captive audience (about 75 others were waiting out the deluge). Let's do it here and now." It was not the way the team planned it, but in God's design the group was still used powerfully that day to lead souls to Christ, right there in that shelter house.

Prayer: Father, direct each of our steps on this short term mission. And, as we prepare to obey You in taking the gospel to many, help me to be sensitive also to the divine appointments here and there, people whom You will bring across my path. As we are careful to plan, lead us in a path that lifts up Your name. And Father, we desire to see an abundant harvest from this mission, and so we set our hands to our preparation, asking You to multiply and extend our impact far beyond that which we could plan or hope for.

DAY 3
LET NO ONE DESPISE YOU

1 Timothy 4:12 *Don't let anyone look down on you because you are young, but set an example for the believers in speech, in life, in love, in faith and in purity.*

Jeremiah 1:5 *"Before I formed you in the womb I knew you; Before you were born I set you apart"*

"I'm only in 10th Grade!"

"I'm a single mother … going on a mission trip?"

"The rest of this team is so young. I'm an old goat!"

"What will this team do with a person of my gender, race, education level, or condition?"

"Why would God want me to be on this team? I can't preach, sing, do mime, and I've never built a building … this makes no sense."

Why DID God call you on this trip? Was it all of your giftedness? Was it your ministry experience? Was it your speaking, musical, theatrical, or construction abilities? Perhaps it was your theological training?

You can be sure that the primary reason you are called to this trip is not any one of those abilities. Your primary qualifications are that God has deposited His presence within your heart and your life, and that you have made yourself available to Him. You may also have some of those other abilities and experiences, and God will use them, but God's passion is for nations to be drawn to HIM. God wants to exhibit Himself to the people He's sending you to and will use an available servant like you, just as you are.

The Apostle Paul once wrote a great letter to a young man named Timothy, recorded in the Scriptures. Paul encouraged him, taught him, and gave him some leadership tips. But then Paul saw a condition in Timothy's life that was beyond his control, something that might affect his confidence: the factor of his youthful age. And Paul said to him, "Don't let anybody put you down because of your age. In fact, don't let anybody even look at you like they are going to put you down over the issue!"

What might be your most limiting factor? Whether it's some physical or natural trait, some experience level, or some life circumstance, hear the voice of the Lord saying to you, "Don't let *anyone* limit you from fulfilling My call on you for that reason! In fact, YOU may be the one looking down on yourself, and it stops right now! I saw that thing about you before I called you, and I still want you. This team needs you; and I want you to carry My presence to this people."

Prayer: Father, thank You that before I was born, You knew me and knew my life circumstances. You set me apart for Your purposes, and I am responding to this stirring that You put in my heart to go to the mission field. Because taking the gospel to the uttermost parts of the earth is Your idea, I resist all temptation to focus on my personal limitations, nor do I care what others who know me might think. I am Your servant, and I trust You and Your call on my life.

DAY 4
HIS LAST WILL AND TESTAMENT

Matthew 28:19 *Go therefore and make disciples of all the nations, baptizing them in the name of the Father and of the Son and of the Holy Spirit*

Luke 24:47 *Repentance and remission of sins should be preached in His name to all nations, beginning at Jerusalem.*

John 20:21 *So Jesus said to them again, "Peace to you! As the Father has sent Me, I also send you."*

Your lawyer can help you write up a "Last Will and Testament." This legal document basically declares your desires, in the event of your death. The one my wife and I filed declares what shall be done with our possessions and with our children. You can declare who your children will be assigned to, and for what purposes your property will be utilized. If you have a will legally recorded, the courts and legal system will support and enforce your wishes with all of their authority, to make sure that your will is executed as written. There is even provision made for an "executor," one who will personally take responsibility for carrying out your desires.

Jesus left us His will and testament. He had it written up and recorded for all generations to witness. He has made provision for His church to serve as "executor" and use all of its authority to execute the desires He expressed in that will.

All four gospels describe Jesus' last words before His ascension. These words in this document tell us what He wants to happen with His children and with His property. His children are to be placed in the care of a local church and be involved in going to the lost with the gospel of Jesus Christ. His things (finances, property, airplanes, buses, and the gifts and power of the Holy Spirit) are to be used to go and advance the good news to all creatures.

You are one of those who are in the process of making sure that His desire is carried out. You are a part of the church, the executor of His will. You are one of His children carrying out His will, and others may be channeling some of His resources, finances, and prayers in your behalf, to assist in the carrying out of His will. It's a tremendous task you are entering into. It wasn't just a good idea you came up with; when you read His testament there was a response in your heart that said, "I'll help carry it out. I'm one of the children He wrote about in that will, and I'm one of those He assigned to a particular people." In this case He is entrusting you with His message, to carry it to those people to whom He is now sending you.

He made no mistakes. You are the perfect one, prepared uniquely for the task He has called you to do. Prepare your heart and be open to His will, and He'll guide you and use you mightily.

Prayer: Lord, I make myself available to You for the carrying out of Your last wishes. I purpose with all my heart to "execute" Your will and testament, which says that I (Your child) and the property You have entrusted to me shall be used to take the gospel to the nations. Prepare my heart for all that You will have for me to do, so that I can help advance the gospel as You commanded in Your Word.

DAY 5
WHY *GOING* IS A GOOD IDEA

Mark 16:15,20 *"Go into all the world and preach the gospel to every creature..." And they went out and preached everywhere, the Lord working with them and confirming the word through the accompanying signs. Amen.*

2 Corinthians 10:4-5 *For the weapons of our warfare are not carnal but mighty in God for pulling down strongholds, casting down arguments and every high thing that exalts itself against the knowledge of God, bringing every thought into captivity to the obedience of Christ,*

In the place you are being sent by the Lord there are spiritual forces of darkness that have been at work in the lives of people who live there. They are not the same evil spirits and forces that are at work where you live. Some spiritual principalities have influenced a whole nation. Others in the hierarchy may be unique to a particular village or neighborhood which you will enter.

You have not been beaten down for years by those spiritual forces that have afflicted the people you are going to meet on the mission field. The people who live where you are going have become so familiar and accustomed to life with the influence of these powers of darkness that they might not even recognize the way evil principalities are influencing their thoughts, lifestyles, and communities.

Likewise when Christian guests come to minister at your church from other parts of the world, they recognize strongholds in our culture that you and I see as "normal" and seem powerless to change (materialism perhaps). They are able to speak into the situation with a clear vision, power and strength, having not been weakened by it themselves their whole life.

There is a reason why very few Old Testament prophets ministered to the people in their own home town community, and why the New Testament commandments also point to a pattern of changing locations? Why? Because there is strategic advantage to actually *going*.

God knew what He was doing when He said "Go." Because you do not reside in the place to which you are being sent, you will sometimes sense certain things about the spiritual "atmosphere." You may recognize dominating territorial spirits at work in the lives of people there (such as spirits of fear, despair, or impurity); in response, you can bring a clear word of faith, hope, and purity.

You will sometimes even feel that you or your mission team are coming under some spiritual attack, when in reality the devil's spiritual forces (which have a stranglehold on the place you are visiting) are trying to put you under the same chains. Instead of thinking you have to fight off these uncommon and strange patterns of thinking, recognize and rejoice that the devil has played his hand. The Holy Spirit is allowing you to see the strong forces of darkness which are at work on your mission field. Now with God's help, you can strategize and receive the message from Him that will set people free from those chains. You can be used by God to set captives free with your words and prayers and actions.

Prayer: Father, give us a sensitivity in our hearts and to Your voice, that we may discover the spiritual forces at work in the lives of those to whom You are sending us. Thank You that the weapons of our warfare (Your truth, Your Holy Spirit, Your Name, and the armor of God) are not feeble but mighty through God for pulling down strongholds. Use us to minister to others by setting them free from the enemy's lies and oppression.

DAY 6
TAKING OTHERS WITH YOU

Philippians 4:17 *"Not that I seek the gift, but I seek the fruit that abounds to your account."*

2 Thessalonians 3:1 *Finally, brethren, pray for us, that the word of the Lord may run swiftly and be glorified, just as it is with you*

Besides those traveling with you on the mission team, you can "take others with you." In fact some people will go on a mission trip as part of a group and in a sense still "go alone." I've done it myself, but only once, and I'll never do it again.

Confused?

I'm speaking of raising support.

"Ohhh. Uughhh. THAT?"

Listen! This is much more than a financial issue. It's a prayer support issue, and if you take the time to generate this support, you will "take people with you" in a way that greatly strengthens you and blesses them.

You may or may not be raising money to undertake this mission, and totally miss something essential. There are two reasons you must involve other people in supporting you, one that benefits them and the other a necessity for you.

1) Do it for them, for the fruit that will come into their lives. My wife and I were the most un-missionary minded people on the planet, until we were asked if we would have a missionary stay at our home one night. We listened while he spoke with us at the dinner table that evening. After that experience we began praying for him regularly, and then started giving money to missions, and God's hand began to touch us deeply. But we would never have actually *gone* ourselves if we'd never first been asked to "go" figuratively by supporting, praying or giving. So by asking others to pray for you, or consider giving to your mission, you are opening doors for God to touch their lives for missions and the nations, to the point that one day they might go as well, or increase in their missions awareness.

2) Do it for yourself, so that the Word of the Lord may run. Do you know that you can have all the money you need for the trip and still be unsupported? You can be "coasting" towards your mission trip because you have your money, while others are sweating it out, working and praying in extra funds to supply for their mission trip. Or, perhaps you are one of those "sweating it out" to raise the finances; it's

possible to have the money come in, and "still not be supported." Here's what I mean: Whether you are "coasting" financially, or you need to raise a lot of finances, your mission trip can impact many more people here and there if you'll give people an opportunity to support you in prayer. Furthermore, if you have a number of faithful Christians praying for you daily you will sense the difference. Let me say it again, "You will FEEL the difference if you have praying believers standing with you in prayer before, during, and just after this mission."

It is important that soon after your decision to participate in a short-term mission, you contact a number of trusted Christians who are faithful and to whom you can say the following: "This is what God had put in my heart to do. I am asking if you would consider praying for me and for this team regularly, beginning today, and continuing until after our return."

Several dynamics will happen. One is that you and the team will be strengthened and this mission will be more fruitful. Also, (and this is the value missionaries like yourself may often overlook) your "partners" will also be touched by God as they talk to Him about your mission. Many people, who are on the mission field today, first went to the mission field on their knees, praying for someone else like you, or supporting someone like you financially. Don't be afraid to ask, and give them an opportunity to begin THEIR missionary journey.

Prayer: Father, cleanse me of any desire to be independent. Show me those friends, neighbors, relatives, or church members whom You would have me involve in this mission by their prayer and financial support. Use this "support-raising" time to strengthen our mission team, and to impact others whose hearts You want to stir to a new level of Kingdom service.

DAY 7
WARNING! BONDING AHEAD!

Philippians 2:3-4 *Let nothing be done through selfish ambition or conceit, but in lowliness of mind let each esteem others better than himself. Let each of you look out not only for his own interests, but also for the interests of others.*

Every short term mission has built into it a motivation for the team members to lean heavily on one another. You are involved in something very adventurous together! During the intensity of a mission trip, people rely on one another at a level that would never happen in the routine of life at home. This dynamic element of the mission causes a healthy bonding to take place.

Now for the WARNING! Being on a short term mission adventure with people of the opposite gender also puts into motion the potential to lean heavily on someone in a way that is UN-healthy. The camaraderie of a team will be severely damaged if two people begin always sitting together at meals and in the vehicles, spending time together and pairing up every chance they can. Listen! Even seasoned and married church leaders have fallen morally on a short term mission. Leaders have personally confided in me about improper bonding that developed on their mission team. It can easily happen when in the strain and stress of working together to face challenges, two people bond into carnal dependence. Though God intends blessing for them, they cross the line into selfish thinking and feed their own lustful desires as the trip progresses.

Safeguards must be put into place up front. Mission leaders I have known from around the world agree that team members must make some decisions before leaving on the trip. One commitment is to accept that their mission is too short a time and too critical for eternal, Kingdom purposes to risk it by pairing up with any "certain person."

Without your full commitment to abstain from any "pairing up," you are not ready to leave for the mission. I am absolutely serious about that: you are not ready to go until you commit.

Team leaders MUST have your permission to hold you accountable in this area. They are responsible to protect the integrity and unity of the group. If God called you to this mission, He called you to consider the group as more important than yourself, and more important than you and "that someone."

Young single man or woman, could God have a future spouse for you right here on your team? Sure, that's possible. But you're going to have to grow together after you're back on home soil where life and its schedules and circumstances are more "normal." Forget any other ideas to the contrary.

Mature married adults, don't think you can't be tempted, so guard yourselves and be open to correction. There is too much at stake.

Prayer: Lord I commit myself to purity and am focusing on this mission and the vision You have for it. I reject all distractions of inappropriate bonding and submit myself totally to my teammates and team leaders for any correction that is needed for the benefit of the team. We're going to serve You and not ourselves. I pray for the entire team and myself that good attitudes and perspective about this issue will prevail.

DAY 8
LET'S CROSS OVER

Mark 4:35-41 *On the same day, when evening had come, He said to them, "Let us cross over to the other side." ... And a great windstorm arose, and the waves beat into the boat, so that it was already filling.*

1 John 4:4 *You are of God, little children, and have overcome them, because He who is in you is greater than he who is in the world.*

Psalm 2:4 *He who sits in the heavens shall laugh; The LORD shall hold them in derision.*

Just a few days before a mission trip to Colombia, South America my entire family broke out with some unusual burning, red spots on our tongues. A trip to the doctor, a prescription, and we all recovered nicely. We never had it before, nor have we ever gotten it since.

The day before another mission trip to Mexico, I accidentally stuck a screwdriver deeply into my face (a long story of stupidity, I assure you). I just missed my eyeball by an eighth of an inch. While blood was pouring down my face, my wife raced me to the doctor and he stitched me up ("Don't move your head" the doctor said as he, without any anesthetic, sewed stitches into the skin next to my eyeball). Then, as we were driving home from the doctor, the exhaust pipe on the van broke, and the muffler dropped out onto the highway below, scraping and breaking. An image of an expensive repair bill appeared in my mind. By then the enemy's attacks had become blatant. My wife was driving while I rode beside her with a blood soaked shirt and an icepack on my face. As the piercing sound of breaking metal pipes scraping the pavement filled our ears, I broke into laughter at the enemy's audacity. "Does the devil think I'm NOT going to go on this mission because of this?"

When Jesus said "Let's go" and you obeyed, you did not receive a free pass from all trouble. In fact, Satan is not too pleased with your decision. Like the disciples who started across the water and encountered "a great windstorm," you may find yourself or your team hit with opposing forces that may attempt to deter the ministry. Even Paul was delayed in coming to Thessalonica for "Satan hindered us" he says.

Your prayer support team is critical; your guard can not be let down. Make sure you arrange for that support and have those people praying before you leave on your trip. Be vigilant, determined, careful, and purposeful. Let your faith arise as the time nears, knowing that "He who is in you is greater than he who is in the world."

Prayer: Lord, we are trusting that You who called us to this missionary endeavor will keep and guard each team member. As the trip nears, we are not unaware that we have a spiritual enemy who would desire to bring harm, but our eyes are on You. We hear the laughter of heaven, that scoffs at the thought that Satan will in any way prevent the fulfillment of Your kingdom purposes, and we rejoice. Praise and honor are due You, Almighty God.

DAY 9
SENT TO THE MANY, BUT DON'T MISS THE ONE!

John 4:3-36 *He left Judea and departed again to Galilee. But He needed to go through Samaria. So He came to a city of Samaria which is called Sychar, near the plot of ground that Jacob gave to his son Joseph. Now Jacob's well was there. Jesus therefore, being wearied from His journey, sat thus by the well. It was about the sixth hour. A woman of Samaria came to draw water. Jesus said to her, "Give Me a drink." ... (later) Jesus said to them (His disciples) "Do you not say, 'There are still four months and then comes the harvest'? Behold, I say to you, lift up your eyes and look at the fields, for they are already white for harvest!"*

Psalm 37:23 *The steps of a good man are ordered by the LORD*

It had been two high stress weeks in Colombia at a time of intense violence in that nation. The schedule had been filled with ministry and exciting opportunities. I was young and inexperienced, but God had used our team and me mightily, and for that a deep satisfaction was settling into my heart. Then, as we were leaving Bogota we had all kinds of problems with airline personnel at the airport over our travel arrangements. After long and tense negotiations, we finally made it on a plane to U.S. soil and were waiting in the Miami airport for a connecting flight to the Midwest.

I was exhausted, experiencing a major "adrenaline let-down," and was looking forward to sleeping on the last leg of the journey. "My mission is over" was my attitude, as we waited at the gate. I watched a mother say goodbye to her teary-eyed small boy who didn't want to let go and take the hand of a flight attendant, who then boarded him on the plane we were about to take. I just noticed it, but thought little of it.

Then it was our turn to board, and where was my assigned seat? Next to that little guy.

I said hello and tried to cheer him up, found out his parents had separated, and that he was leaving Mom to visit Dad who moved to another state. He was flying for the first time in his little life…alone. Scared to death, his stomach became sickened as the plane took flight, adding to his misery and shame.

… "Wait, little English speaking American boys weren't on the prayer list! He didn't look anything like the Colombians for whom we had prepared and been ministering to. I'm tired now, finished. I want to sleep! The trip is over." But

God has us on a mission EVERY step of the way. That boy was there for me to minister to.

On another mission trip, Jesus was just traveling, not ministering to any crowds, "passing through Samaria," when his disciples went into town to get lunch at the nearest McDonalds. Jesus rested on the outskirts. He wasn't purposing to touch a crowd that day, but when a woman came by the well, He ministered to her at her point of need. Through her a whole village was reached. Never say, "When we get there I'm a missionary," or "Now that we've left, I'm NOT a missionary." You are the Lord's servant every day and moment of your life. You may be sent to multitudes on this mission trip, but don't miss the one along the way, for whom Jesus also died.

Prayer: Lord thank You for sending me to this special people, but help me, as I and my team prepare and travel, to notice the one here and the one there, that You bring across my steps every day. Don't let me miss what You are doing every moment of my life. My times are in Your hands, so I surrender my agenda and needs to You. Use me as You see fit.

DAY 10
MIRACULOUS PROTECTION AND
TRAVELING MERCY

Psalm 34:7 *The angel of the LORD encamps all around those who fear Him, And delivers them.*

Luke 18:1-8 *One day Jesus told his disciples a story to illustrate their need for constant prayer and to show them that they must never give up. ... don't you think God will surely give justice to his chosen people who plead with him day and night? Will he keep putting them off? I tell you, he will grant justice to them quickly!*

Psalm 127:1 *Unless the LORD guards the city, the watchman stays awake in vain.*

Our team had been traveling cramped in a 15 passenger van for four weeks. We ministered in southern Mexico immediately following a devastating earthquake and were making our way back north to the U.S. This mission group included some married team members, two one-year old babies, another small child, and some singles. Two large luggage racks were braced to the top of the van and piled high with suitcases and bags, making for quite an eye-catching (and sometimes humorous) sight as we crossed the Mexican landscape. We may have looked much like the Beverly Hillbillies did on their way to California.

Part way back to the U.S. we stopped to fill up the van at a gas station, when the van refused to start up and go again. A couple of men on the team had some mechanical experience, and tried a multitude of things to get it going, but without luck; the engine simply refused to start.

The team was hot, dirty, frustrated, and perplexed about what to do next. But instinctively, we did what Christians always ought to do: we joined together and prayed. As the "amen" sounded, one of the men felt a nudging in his heart to get down and "look under the van at the gas tank."

Being a mechanic, this made no sense to him, but he obeyed. When he did, he saw nothing around the gas tank that appeared wrong, but as he was about to get back up, an apple-sized bulge on the inside wall of a rear tire glared at him. The horror of it was evident: if the team had continued down the highway at 60 mph, that bulging tire would most certainly have exploded, tossing the top-heavy van on its side in a tragic accident. The men changed the tire, and then … guess what? The van engine started right up, never to trouble the group again.

Present the issue of your safety and protection to your prayer partners as you undertake this mission, and always keep the need before the Lord in your own prayers as well, never taking it for granted.

Prayer: Lord, unless You guard our team, we have no protection, but with Your protection, we are completely safe from any attack of the evil one. We confess our need of Your divine, complete, and angelic protection on this mission trip, and commit every facet of the trip earnestly to Your shield of protection. Keep us, guide us, and guard us from all harm.

SPECIAL DAY OF PRAYER AND FASTING FOR YOUR TEAM

1 Peter 5:6-7 *Therefore humble yourselves under the mighty hand of God, that He may exalt you in due time, casting all your care upon Him, for He cares for you.*

Philippians 4:6 *Be anxious for nothing, but in everything by prayer and supplication, with thanksgiving, let your requests be made known to God*

Today, take some extra time to pray more specifically for your short term mission team. Your group might be four people, or it might be 44 people; either way, use the spaces below to name team members for whom you are going to pray today. Consider how the Lord would have you fast (all day, one meal) and pray.

Look back over the devotionals you've read so far and see if the Lord would want you to review specific points and focus more concerted prayer about a particular day's message and its impact on you. Are there specific issues or practical prayer needs that your team has discussed, about which you can spend some focused time praying? Or are there particular issues that you have been uneasy about? Are there specific team members that you are aware of that may be struggling for some reason (finances, health, family issues, other needs)? Right now, lift those concerns to the Lord and let Him carry them for you, and let's see what He will do!

_____ Team leader

_____ Team members _____

_____   _____

_____   _____

_____   _____

_____   _____

_____   _____

_____   _____

_____   _____

_____   _____

_____   _____

Issues of concern the team has discussed: _____

_____

_____

Issues about which I have been uneasy, or team members who may be struggling: _____

_____

_____

Is there a particular prayer assignment that you can give to a particular friend who will be faithful to intercede for you and your team?

DAY 11
TEAM UNITY

Philippians 2:2 *"Fulfill my joy by being like minded, having the same love, being of one accord, of one mind."*

Ephesians 4:16 *the whole Body, joined and knit together by what every joint supplies*

I've watched sports over the years, and I marvel at how a team with less talent and skill will often overcome the superior skills of another team and defeat them.

How can that be?

Usually that which puts the less skilled team "over the top" is their "team spirit." The successful coach builds the group together in such a way that they are able to do more as a cohesive unit than another group of more highly skilled athletes can do if they play as a bunch of ego-driven individuals.

The same is true of your mission group. Don't underestimate the value of pre-trip training and mission team meetings. Take every opportunity to be together as a group before the short term mission. Share your heart, your emotions, your prayer requests, your financial needs, your spiritual battles. Pray for one another, get to know one another, build each other up, and practice being together.

You need them, and they need you. In fact, the Bible says in Ephesians 4 that the Body of Christ is joined and knit together by that which every person supplies. Eternity is at stake for someone you minister to, and the team will be less effective and less fruitful if any one person fails to fulfill their role on the mission.

Going from the familiarity of normal life to the less familiar experience of the mission is an opportunity for each person to trust God in a deeper way. This is especially true if each team member has come to know and trust the love of each person on the team. Knowing the love, acceptance, and support of the group frees individuals to move in their personal gifting. Yet such trust and love takes time to develop. Building unity during team preparation is also important because the enemy of our souls will often attack team unity on the mission.

It seems like a squeeze in our tight life schedules to add "team meetings" to the calendar, as if it is a "necessary evil" of the short term mission experience. Reject that attitude, and recognize that the ministry has already begun, and part of that ministry is building together as a unit.

Prayer: Lord thank You for that which each team member brings to this group. I purpose, by Your grace, to walk in love with each team member. Father, build us together, unite us in purpose, and draw out of us the unique quality and gifting You put in us for the benefit of the group.

DAY 12
THREE THINGS GOD
SAYS TO HIS KIDS

Galatians 3:26 *For you are all sons of God through faith in Christ Jesus.*

Jeremiah 31:3 ... *"Yes, I have loved you with an everlasting love; Therefore with lovingkindness I have drawn you.*

Matthew 3:17 *And suddenly a voice came from heaven, saying, "This is My beloved Son, in whom I am well pleased."*

When Jesus came out of the waters of baptism, a voice from heaven proclaimed: "This is My beloved Son, in whom I am well pleased." These words were ringing in His mind and heart as he embarked on the next 40 days of testing in the wilderness and as He began His earthly ministry in the power of the Holy Spirit.

In today's devotional, you need to hear the Father say these same things over you, so the words will be ringing in your ears as you embark on your mission to the field. If you truly hear this, you will receive the same strength in your soul for the unknown journey ahead and the same power for your ministry.

1. "You are my child." In the world, it has happened that many men have left a woman whom they made pregnant; he disappears, taking no responsibility. But in the kingdom of heaven, God says "I will never deny you! I will never shirk responsibility for you! You are MY child. I claim you as My own." Your identity is wrapped up in whose child you are, and who is your Father.

2. "You are my beloved." Nobody can love you like God can. And He does love you unconditionally, eternally, and with more affection than any earthly parent can possibly bestow.

3. "With you, I am well pleased." Perhaps you've heard the previous two statements before, and have accepted the idea that God loves you and that you are His child. But will you also accept and embrace this third one? "With you I am well pleased."

You think, "Doesn't He know where I've been? I know my failures, my lack of self discipline; they are all too much in the forefront of my thinking and awareness." God says that you have received His mercy; He sees you through the lens of His Son's perfect nature. And today, through the lens of the cross and Jesus' blood, the Father sees the humble one who acknowledges a need for His grace and He says to you "I am well pleased with you."

Open your heart and hear it again: "This is My beloved son (or daughter), in whom I am well pleased."

Prayer: Oh, God, I find strength for the road ahead as I hear Your voice saying that I am Your child, that You love me, and that I please You. Hallelujah! I may find those statements incredible, but because You say them, and because Your blood and grace have cleansed me, I believe them to be true. In fact, I relish the thoughts. Thank You for accepting me and embracing me as Yours. Your grace has enabled me to find my way to this point, and You are the One who will carry me through temptation and danger and the coming mission trip that's ahead.

DAY 13
AS YOU ARE GOING, HE LEADS

Mark 16:15 *Go into all the world and preach the gospel to every creature.*

Acts 16:6-10 *Now when they had gone through Phrygia and the region of Galatia, they were forbidden by the Holy Spirit to preach the word in Asia. After they had come to Mysia, they tried to go into Bithynia, but the Spirit did not permit them. So passing by Mysia, they came down to Troas. And a vision appeared to Paul in the night. A man of Macedonia stood and pleaded with him, saying, "Come over to Macedonia and help us." Now after he had seen the vision, immediately we sought to go to Macedonia, concluding that the Lord had called us to preach the gospel to them.*

God speaks in many ways, so the manner in which you ended up a part of this mission team could differ greatly from the way others found themselves on it with you. Sometimes, God directs you in very dramatic ways. Other times, it's a gentle nudging in your heart from God that He wants you to go. And then sometimes, you don't have a sense that God "spoke" to you; you just feel a desire to go and the door opens wide!

One of the most dramatic directional missionary experiences recorded in the Bible is when God called Paul to Macedonia. He saw a vision in the night "Come over to Macedonia and help us."

Wow, now THAT would give you confidence, wouldn't it, if God gave you a vision to participate in your particular short term mission?

Notice that Paul wasn't sitting at home when the dramatic direction came to him. Paul was just obeying God's general command to "go into all the world," which is the Great Commission given to us all. Paul was so dedicated to that mission, that even without any specific direction from the Lord, he set out to go into Asia. As he was going, God said "no," but Paul didn't stop. He just said, "OK, I'll try Bithynia." As he was going, the Lord said "no" again. Paul still didn't stop, but kept going until the shores of the sea stopped him near Troas. I'm sure that by this time Paul was doing some serious praying. Then, he received the dramatic vision and historic call, one which turned the general direction of the gospel to Europe and the West. This dramatic call was not Paul's first missionary endeavor, nor was it his last.

There's something important for you to understand as a short term missionary: you are responding to the will of God in your efforts to take the gospel to other parts of the world. If you need a dramatic intervention to direct you as you go, God knows where you are, and can speak to you in a way that you'll know He's talking to you. But in the meantime, God is pleased with your faithful obedience to His general commission spoken to all believers.

Be open to the possibility that, as you go on this short term mission, God may give you a key that will open more doors for missions in the future. This may be a stepping stone to other places and nations that still haven't crossed your mind. It may even be possible that as your team pursues the current plan, God may adjust that plan in surprising ways ... but as you go. So, keep going!

Prayer: Father, I join my heart to the words of Your command, that we be about the work of taking the gospel to every creature in every place. I hear Your heart that beats for the nations, and respond with a desire to go. As I go, I know that this is only one step on a lifelong journey of obedience, and ask for Your direction every step, and at every turn. Help me always have a hearing ear. I lean upon You to guide, direct, open doors, or even close doors if need be, to help me fulfill my part in the Great Commission.

DAY 14
SSSTTTRETCH MARKS

Hebrews 11:6,8 *But without faith it is impossible to please Him, for he who comes to God must believe that He is, and that He is a rewarder of those who diligently seek Him... By faith Abraham obeyed when he was called to go out to the place which he would receive as an inheritance.*

Every short term mission should stretch your faith. It's not life as usual. It's being part of something bigger than you. It's a move from the familiar to the unfamiliar, and to the unknown.

What happens when life consists of the same routine every day? Well, if you are like me, you can get careless and lethargic in your relationship to God, because you at least think you know what's coming.

But when the routine is broken, as it is about to be when you leave on this trip, there is an interesting dynamic that kicks into gear, a new urgency to rely on God. The short term missionary embarks on an adventure that's more than a change in geography. You have no choice but to trust in God moment by moment in ways you would never have to if all was familiar. When you go from the familiar to the unfamiliar your faith is forced to grow more active. And because God responds to faith, guess what? You experience Him in new ways in your life.

As you step out into new territory, the Lord will often step up the intensity in which a spiritual gift operates in your life (it may even have been dormant inside you up to now). While on the unfamiliar terrain of a mission you will listen to the voice of the Holy Spirit with greater care and sensitivity than you typically would during the normal routine. You may be asked to do something that is not routine for you, like speaking or giving testimony publicly, or praying for the sick. You may face some practical challenge that is completely new to you. You may need to make a decision in the course of the trip, a decision which taps undeveloped leadership potential in you. Unexpected circumstances could tap certain skills in you that nobody else knew you had. In a spot like that you will find yourself desperately leaning on Christ and experiencing His wonderful help in ways you never have before. You are now right where God wants you. Now, He can reveal more of Himself, and more of His great power, in you and through you. The team can pull together to accomplish more than the sum of what each of you can do individually. Because you're obeying the Great Commission, God's anointing will be strong in you. The Lord will use you.

Expect a fresh touch from God as you prepare and participate in the mission. As the trip approaches, prepare your heart by taking extended time with the Lord, communing with him. Consider fasting for a period of time. Expect great things from God!

Prayer: Thank you, Lord, for calling me to be a part of something bigger than myself, and for calling me to seek eternal fruit in a place and environment unfamiliar to me. You are the God to whom I look for provision, guidance, grace, power, and anointing to enjoy a successful mission. I consecrate my life to Your use, and trust You to draw out of me gifts and potential that I may not currently be using to the fullest.

DAY 15
WHEN JESUS SAYS "FOLLOW ME" A SECOND TIME

Matthew 4:18-19 *And Jesus, walking by the Sea of Galilee, saw two brothers, Simon called Peter, and Andrew his brother, casting a net into the sea; for they were fishermen. Then He said to them, "Follow Me, and I will make you fishers of men."*

John 21:18-19 *"Most assuredly, I say to you, when you were younger, you girded yourself and walked where you wished; but when you are old, you will stretch out your hands, and another will gird you and carry you where you do not wish...Follow Me."*

The leaders of your mission will sometimes ask you to do things and go places you would not have naturally chosen. You'll wonder "Why, if I'm following the Lord's leading, is my missionary leader, host, or guide, asking me to do this? This is not me!"

Simon Peter heard the words "Follow Me" at least twice, according to the gospel accounts. The first time was when Jesus first called him to be a disciple. In response, he left his fishing boat behind and followed the Lord, his life to change forever. When Jesus said it a second time, He added that if Peter was to continue following Him, others were going to take him to places and circumstances that he wouldn't naturally choose.

After hearing the first "Follow Me," Peter became a disciple, saw the miracles, experienced God's goodness, was taught of the Lord, participated in ministry himself, asked questions, and grew in the things of the kingdom. He wasn't perfect, speaking by the Holy Spirit at times, speaking from the flesh at others.

In the same way, you may have answered the first "Follow Me" when you gave your life to Christ. Between then and now you've grown, been taught, and experienced God's goodness. Perhaps you have been involved in some types of ministry, and seen the power of God in answer to prayer.

The question is, have you answered the call to "Follow Me" in the way Jesus expressed it to Peter the second time? For Peter, it happened three years later, just before the Lord's ascension. After three years of following Jesus, the Lord said it again.

You see, despite everything Peter had experienced in those three years, he still had preconceived ideas about how the kingdom of God should be run ("No Lord, never" he had recently

said as Jesus explained what would soon happen).
In presenting this second "Follow Me" Jesus says
that Peter still has a lot of independence left in his
life. "You girded yourself and walked where you
wished; but when you are old" or, in other words
"sometime in the future, you will lose so much of
your independence that other people will take you
where you would not choose to go". Jesus promised that "others" would take Peter against his
will all the way to his martyrdom. When others
were taking him some place difficult, Jesus said
that, even then, he was following God.

Jesus said "Follow Me" to you and then handed
you off to some human Christian leaders and said,
"To follow Me, you are going to have to serve in
what they ask you to do. The day you quit doing
what they ask, no matter what a death it is to your
agenda, you've quit following Me." Continue
following the Lord by faithfully following the
leaders He puts in your life now. It's a remarkable
new life of surrender you'll enter into.

Prayer: Lord, I lift my hands and heart in
surrender, not simply volunteering to serve
You in ways I choose, or presuming to know
exactly how You will accomplish Your purposes.
I release preconceived ideas and personal preferences. Take me where You wish, as I submit
to those You place over me, doing what they, in
Your sovereign plan, set before me.

DAY 16
MIGRANT WORKERS FOR JESUS

John 4:35 *Do you not say, 'There are still four months and then comes the harvest'? Behold, I say to you, lift up your eyes and look at the fields, for they are already white for harvest!*

Growing up in Northwest Ohio, I saw many migrant workers from Mexico arrive in the summer time and help farmers harvest their vegetables. Tomatoes, cucumbers and other crops could never have been brought in without their help.

One of my mission groups was doing evangelistic work with a national pastor overseas. God had done miracles that day, opening more opportunities to share the gospel than any of us could have expected. Many people had responded and wanted to be saved. The pastor and the team had prayed for hours with those spiritually hungry people, souls desiring to begin their walk with Jesus Christ. After the day's ministry, the team decided "Let's stop for some ice cream and celebrate this great day God has given us." As the team celebrated, I noticed that the international pastor was having a tough time entering into the happiness.

"Pastor, you seem heavy hearted," I remarked. "What is the matter?"

"I am so thankful for the team and rejoice with them, but I AM heavy hearted. There are so many of my people who are ready to receive Jesus as their Savior, if only they hear the news. I am heavy hearted for my people, not wanting any of them to die without hearing the gospel."

I remembered those farmers back in Ohio, and thought of how they would have felt if they had plowed, planted seed, fertilized, weeded, and nurtured their crops, only to have them rot in the fields because there weren't enough hands to help with the harvest. Imagine how sick in heart such a farmer would feel, watching ripened crops rot!

This pastor was feeling that way, only in this case not about vegetables, but about eternal souls! He saw that there is a tremendous harvest ripe and ready now, and he felt that some souls might be lost forever without enough hands to help in the labor.

God has sent you, like a "spiritual migrant worker" to help local "farmers" in God's harvest fields. You're being sent to help because it's harvest time; stay focused, work hard, and be an encouragement wherever you go.

Prayer: God, there is work to be done in another place, and You are sending me there.

Make me an encouragement to the national workers, and as spiritual "migrant workers" we lend our hands to You and to them, in this great harvest field. Use us mightily, I pray, to help make sure that none for whom Your love is reaching out are lost. Help us to be effective and thorough.

DAY 17
LIONS AND TIGERS AND BEARS ...
AND MORE

Mark 1:12-13 *Immediately the Holy Spirit compelled Jesus to go into the wilderness. He was there for forty days, being tempted by Satan. He was out among the wild beasts, and angels took care of him.*

Psalm 91:11 *For He shall give His angels charge over you, To keep you in all your ways.*

Will God only lead you to safe places to minister on this trip? Some of the most difficult days of Jesus' life were the forty He spent fasting in the wilderness. The Bible does not say "Then Jesus made a big mistake and walked into the wilderness where He became lost and suffered the consequences." Nor does it say that He messed up and was thrown into the wilderness as punishment for some sin. On the contrary, it says that the "Holy Spirit compelled Jesus" or "led Jesus" or "sent Jesus" (depending on which translation) into the wilderness for 40 days.

In those 40 days, Jesus was without food, alone, in a desolate place.

Actually, you may have noticed that Jesus was NOT really alone. The Bible mentions others that were present. There was Satan, who tempted and tested Him. The Bible usually does not waste words; it also mentions that there were wild beasts present with Jesus.

We know from history that in those days there were wild boars, jackals, foxes, leopards, hyenas, and wolves living in the region. The mention of "wild beasts" in Scripture indicates that there would have been some very real natural danger to a man in the wild.

But there was one more set of unseen companions there with Jesus: angels (plural) that "took care of Him." Imagine angels of God helping you and caring for you.

So, while being led by the Holy Spirit to this harsh environment with difficult living conditions and danger around every hill and crevice, the devil severely tested Him, but angels took care of Him.

Sometimes the Holy Spirit leads you into places with the gospel that don't look safe in the natural, but the truth is that there is no safer place than where God sends you. You could find yourself on some inner city street on a dark night, in a nation with a government hostile to Christians, in one of the many places on the earth filled with literal wild beasts or dangerous bugs, or in a culture that looks down on your skin color. These are only some of the risks that following the Lord might expose you to. But there too, among the wild beasts and among the devils, you are not alone facing them. There are the angels of God with you, taking care of you!

Prayer: Give us wisdom so that we might not willingly or unwittingly expose ourselves to potential harm. But ultimately it is You we rely on for our safety. As we follow Your leading, my teammates and I rest safely in Your protective hands. Let Your angels care and serve and look after our way. Thanks for these unseen angels You have provided us as companions and ministering spirits.

DAY 18
DO YOU LIKE MY COUNTRY?

Psalm 24:1 *The earth is the LORD's, and all its fullness, the world and those who dwell therein.*

Proverbs 25:11 *A word fitly spoken is like apples of gold in settings of silver.*

Proverbs 25:25 *As cold water to a weary soul, So is good news from a far country.*

It's an innocent question, isn't it? "Do you like my country?" Or "What do you think of my church? Is it okay?"

The questions are filled with potential traps for you and are born out of heart-rending worries by those who are asking. Some missionaries and travelers are highly honored for no other reason than that they have traveled so far to come, or just because the country of their origin is respected so highly. To illustrate their approach to your visit in some places, imagine hosting a state governor in your home. You would get the land-scape manicured and the house cleaned before the entourage arrived, wouldn't you? For some precious people of simple means, your visit to them is as significant as a State Governor's visit to your house would be.

I've been in nations where I was never allowed to hand carry any of my bags or belongings anywhere. People would literally insist on carrying my Bible to my seat in the church, lest they somehow fail in being sufficiently hospitable.

This *may* not become your experience, depending on the nation you are visiting and what the local perceptions of you or your nationality are, and depending on their cultural approach to visitors. Some cultures actually prefer to remain to themselves or are indifferent to outsiders; others are outright hostile to the gospel.

But if it does become your experience, handling such hospitality and honor with grace can be difficult. When I consider the hardships Christians go through in many of the places I've visited, and as I consider the sacrifices they are making for the Lord, the question "What do you think of my church?" evokes my own question. "What place of esteem do I hold to be allowed to answer such a question? You are amazing people of great faith! Would to God that we had the strengths YOU have!"

What's really being asked of us visitors by such questions? I believe that the core issue tugging at their heart is "Am I okay?" In many places where communication and media are limited, people have heard stories about where you are from, but their perspective on themselves is so limited. They may be struggling for survival in their geographic area, travel little, have limited interaction with Christians from other churches, and seriously wonder "How do we measure up?" They may have little to compare themselves to.

So be ready, not to issue a comparison or an evaluation, but a word of encouragement! Take time to ponder and discuss with your team what strengths of character God has put into the lives of your hosts. Look for the beauty God has put in the country; after all, the creation is His, even the starkest parts of the planet. The earth is full of His glory, so notice it as you go. Be ready to express these things as words of encouragement.

Prayer: Father, help me appreciate the God-created beauty of my host country, that I might see Your handiwork in the land, the culture, and the people. Give me eyes to see Your image expressed in the lives of the people You love and are sending me to. Make me a channel of encouragement and affirmation wherever I can express Your kindness. Let my life bring refreshing "water" to the dry places.

DAY 19
AMBASSADORS FOR CHRIST, NOT "UGLY WESTERNERS"

2 Corinthians 5:20 *We are therefore Christ's ambassadors, as though God were making his appeal through us.*

I was so horrified I felt like disassociating myself from the team. We just left a ministry site in a needy neighborhood after a morning of ministering to children, when a half mile down the dirt street from the church, I saw in the rear-view mirror a kind-hearted brother throwing dollar bills out our van window. His actions caused a mob of children to run after and along side the van, fighting and climbing over each other in the street grasping for cash. We still had some distance to go to be out of this crowded and dangerous area of the city, I couldn't drive fast on the dirt street (especially with children running right along the wheels), and some unseemly characters were now giving this strange "money van" their full attention.

"Does this flamboyance advance the gospel?"

Face it. Peoples from around the world get stereotyped. You hear that someone from another country is visiting, and certain characteristics come to mind. It's really unfortunate when a

Christian goes abroad and acts in a way more fitting of some national stereotype than his or her spiritual family.

People from North America are often stereotyped as "Ugly Americans"; Westerners in general evoke an image in many parts of the world. It's no wonder: loudness, flamboyance, arrogance, insensitivity, exploiting the poor for a "photo op," voicing our displeasure with the bathroom conditions, flippantly tossing money around (even in charity). These are just a few ways that our cultural "behavior" might offend others. Try as we might, even seasoned short-termers have blown it.

The Bible is sprinkled with many sayings about our true spiritual identity (about who we are in Christ). Being a "child of God," the "righteousness of God" and "more than conquerors" are just a few. One of our challenges on any mission is to walk in a manner worthy of that true identity we have as the Lord's representatives.

If I attend a government-held public meeting in my local community to state my opinions, I can say what I want. But if I attend that public meeting as a representative of my employer, I am no longer free to be selfish. I must speak from the perspective of my company's best interests.

The key to being an ambassador for Christ is to keep His interests our priority. Reflect his nature, stay focused on Christ in conversation, and minister with a spirit of humility. Consider others more important than ourselves, remembering His interest being the souls for whom He gave His blood. Offense usually happens when we start to get a little "comfortable" with the national Christians who are hosting us, or our interpreter, or someone we are ministering to, and we forget the One we represent. Our calling, as an ambassador, is to walk in a manner worthy of the One who called us. His life is one of humility, compassion, understanding, mercy, holiness, gratitude, meekness, service, and honor. Let's reflect that life.

Prayer: Lord, I'm going on this mission because You are sending me. Thank You for allowing me to carry Your message and presence. By Your grace, I endeavor to consider others more important than myself. Let my life represent You, reflect Your truth and compassion, for I go as Your ambassador.

DAY 20
FLESH VS. SPIRIT

Galatians 5: 17, 22 *"For the flesh wars against spirit, and the spirit against the flesh; and these are contrary to one another...But the fruit of the spirit is love."*

Encountering spiritual opposition on a mission trip is commonplace. Spiritual warfare training should be a part of every short term mission team's preparation. After all, your spiritual enemy is not happy that you responded to God's command to take the gospel into all the world.

But often in team ministry, the most difficult warfare encountered seems "internal."

That person on the team whose personality "bugs you" prior to the trip? The thing they do that gets under your skin? Guess what? They'll bug you more when you're together all day, every day! It's easier to overlook those issues when you only see them in church on Sunday morning. When you are with them 24/7, day after day... it gets tough to endure.

"Uh, oh, you're right! I better start praying that they will change quickly!"

Nice try! The issue is not their need to change, but it is YOU and your flesh.

Yes, each of us can "put on the armor of God" to protect ourselves against the devil. This armor, however, will not cover and protect the flesh.

Picture a large person, if you will, wearing armor that is lean and tight. The flesh that can't fit inside the armor is vulnerable to enemy arrows. Your un-crucified flesh is an open target that the devil has permission to shoot at. If you want to focus on the other person's weaknesses, faults and personality quirks more than you want to seek God's help to walk in love towards them, you have some serious internal warfare in store for you. Instead of letting yourself be a vulnerable target for the enemy while the things other team members do "push your buttons," disconnect the buttons from your life by going to the Lord in brokenness and confession.

Depend on Him for an outpouring of His love in your heart. Cry out to God for more of the love He has in His heart for your teammates. Be aggressive and fervent about this in prayer. If you must, confess to a trusted leader that you need him or her to pray for you about this and confess that you don't want your flesh getting in the way of a victory over what "bugs" you.

Prayer: Lord, I confess my need of You. Every good gift comes from You, so I make a willful decision to embrace with thanksgiving the circumstances of this mission. I humble myself before Your mighty hand, and surrender all independence. I thank You for every member of this team and ask for the love of God for each of my team members. Concerning any of those characteristics in team members that have in any way irritated me, I ask Your forgiveness for seeing them only "in the flesh" and wishing they were different. Lord, it's MY heart that needs Your touch. With Your help I put away selfish thinking and choose to embrace my teammates as You see them, gifts chosen for this mission to advance the Kingdom of Heaven.

SPECIAL DAY OF PRAYER AND FASTING FOR YOUR LOGISTICS

Psalm 37:23 *The steps of a good man are ordered by the LORD, And He delights in his way.*

Philippians 4:6 *Be anxious for nothing, but in everything by prayer and supplication, with thanksgiving, let your requests be made known to God.*

Today, take some extra time to pray more specifically for your short term mission trip and its practical arrangements. Consider again how the Lord would have you fast (all day, one meal).

Look back over the devotionals you've read so far and see if the Lord would want you to review specific points and focus more concerted prayer about a particular devotional. Are there specific issues or practical prayer needs that your team has discussed, about which you can spend some focused time praying? Or are there particular issues that you have been uneasy about? Right now, lift those concerns to the Lord and let Him carry them for you; let's see what He will do!

_____ Team leader

_____ Location we are headed

_____ Primary type of
work for this team

Prayer checklist:

_____ Travel to the host nation or location
_____ In country travel arrangements once there
_____ The safety of the team
_____ God's favor on the team
_____ The food we will be eating
_____ Team health
_____ Host site(s) where the team will be staying
_____ Language barriers / interpreters
_____ Adjustment to the climate, culture, and conditions

Issues of concern the team has discussed: _____

_____
_____

Issues I have been uneasy or worried about:

_____
_____

Is there a particular prayer assignment that you can give to a particular friend who will be faithful to intercede for you and your team?

DAY 21
SIGNS AND WONDERS ARE FOLLOWING YOU

Mark 16:14-20 *Later He appeared to the eleven as they sat at the table; and He rebuked their unbelief and hardness of heart, because they did not believe those who had seen Him after He had risen. And He said to them, "Go into all the world and preach the gospel to every creature. He who believes and is baptized will be saved; but he who does not believe will be condemned. And these signs will follow those who believe: In My name they will cast out demons; they will speak with new tongues; they will take up serpents; and if they drink anything deadly, it will by no means hurt them; they will lay hands on the sick, and they will recover."*

So then, after the Lord had spoken to them, He was received up into heaven, and sat down at the right hand of God. And they went out and preached every-where, the Lord working with them and confirming the word through the accom-panying signs. Amen.

Ever play "Follow the Leader," or irritate someone by repeating what they say?

The truth is that we all know *how* to follow someone. It's just a matter of whether or not we *choose* to follow them.

It's also the truth that you can't repeat someone's words if they don't say something, nor can you follow someone who is not moving.

The Bible says that when you, as a believer, go into all the world and preach the gospel, that signs will follow you.

When you play "Follow the Leader" you have confidence that as you walk, the other person is following you. When someone is repeating everything you say (irritating as it might be), you know that the next thing out of your mouth will be repeated by the other. God has made a promise to you that when you go bearing the good news, something will be right behind you following after you. That "something" is the presence and power of the resurrected and living God. He promised to manifest Himself on behalf of the message you testify to.

As you go on a mission trip, there will be more spiritual activity both in opposition to your movements, and in support of them. Thankfully, "greater is He who is in you than he who is in the world."

We often wonder why we don't see more Bible-like miracles in our "normal" lives, but then, the Bible says the signs will "follow." This means that we have to be moving, not standing still, in order to be followed! It's impossible for miracle signs to "follow" if no one is going anywhere!

You, however, ARE going somewhere in obedience to the Lord's commission. So as you go on this trip, remember to expect a "following." Remember who and what it is you should expect following your every move: miracles, the presence and protection of God, and the power of the Holy Spirit. Believe it and thank God for it!

Prayer: Lord, I thank You that as we go to take the gospel to the nations, You go with us to confirm Your message with signs and miracles. When our protection is at stake, You will be faithful to look after us. When it is power that's needed, we thank You for the gifts of the Holy Spirit that work in us, and will work through us. As we proclaim Your name, Jesus, may there be a trail behind us … a trail of changed lives that brings honor to Your powerful name.

DAY 22
A KEY TO MINISTERING
WITH AUTHORITY

Luke 10:18 *"Behold I give you the authority to trample on serpents and scorpions, and over all the power of the enemy, and nothing will by any means hurt you."*

Matthew 8:8-10 *The centurion answered and said, "Lord, I am not worthy that You should come under my roof. But only speak a word, and my servant will be healed. For I also am a man under authority, having soldiers under me. And I say to this one, 'Go,' and he goes; and to another, 'Come,' and he comes; and to my servant, 'Do this,' and he does it."*

When Jesus heard it, He marveled, and said to those who followed, "Assuredly, I say to you, I have not found such great faith, not even in Israel!

When Jesus marvels at something, we ought to really take notice! Think of it: the Son of God, the Savior of the world, the Lord of the heavens, in Matthew Chapter 8, is said to have "marveled" at a person's faith. He then says to the other people present, "I have not found such great faith, not even in Israel."

The man whose faith captured the Lord's attention in this way was a Roman Centurion, a military man whose servant was paralyzed in a terrible condition. When Jesus offered to go to the servant the centurion sent word "only speak a word, and my servant will be healed, for I too am a man under authority, and I say to this one 'go here' and he goes."

The Centurion didn't say "I too am a man WITH authority," but "I too am a man UNDER authority." He recognized a truth about authority that we need to get into our hearts. He saw Jesus exercise authority over demons and sickness and knew that it had to be because Jesus was submitted to an authority of a greater and heavenly power. He knew that his own authority to command soldiers under him was only effective because he was under and submitted to those over him in the chain of command.

It is like a police officer. The officer carries authority to command or even arrest you, and he carries a badge authorizing him to do so. If that officer should disobey orders from his commanding officer, then he will lose both his badge and his authority to command and arrest you.

Likewise, if the centurion was to begin "doing his own thing" and not obeying those over him, he'd be stripped of any authority to command soldiers under him.

Do you want to minister in the authority of God? God has made His "badge" of spiritual authority over demonic powers available to every believer. Remain *under* authority, submitted to God and to the human and Christian authorities he has placed over you. Do your own thing independently, and you lose God's authority. Remain under the leaders He blessed you with on this mission trip. Only then (when u*nder* God and His leadership) can you be confident that you *have* authority over all the powers of darkness

Prayer: God I submit to Your Lordship in my life, and to those You've placed over me. Rid me of every independent tendency. Oh Lord thank You that, in Christ, You have raised me from the dead and seated me together with Christ in heavenly places, far above all powers of the enemy. In confidence, then, and with boldness, I take authority over the enemy and his works in the lives of others to whom You are sending me, and carry Your anointing to break powers of darkness off of their lives.

DAY 23
LOSING TO GOD WILL HELP
YOU WIN

James 4:6-7 *But He gives more grace. Therefore He says "God resists the proud, but gives grace to the humble." Therefore submit to God.*

It happens frequently on a short term mission team. For no obvious reason two people on the team are having very different experiences. Every one on the team is involved in a great work for God. They completed the same application and took the same immunizations. They prepared together, prayed together, traveled together, are staying in the same housing, using the same showers, riding the same planes, buses, or vans, and eating the same food.

Outwardly they are not having "different experiences" at all. But look at them! One is having the time of his life. The other? Miserable as can be.

Some men on a construction team in Mexico were once struggling with the hot and arid climate, the dust, the altitude, and the different building methods being used (which they were not accustomed to). As tensions built, the guys began grumbling and getting on one another's nerves. Off to one side, one of the only two girls on the team was working quietly (on necessary stuff none of the guys wanted to do, by the way). She spoke up to me, but loud enough for everyone to hear: "I love this mission trip. I love this team, this place, this church we're serving, the Mexican people, and this job I was asked to do! I wouldn't be anywhere else in the world!"

You could have heard a pin drop among the big tough men who had been grumbling in their hearts. They had been humbled by a girl who was enjoying what they were not, and they were under the conviction of the Holy Spirit.

What is the reason that one can be so happy and another so miserable? Why does one have grace to endure the new culture and the other doesn't? Why does one enjoy the opportunity to relate to other teammates and the other doesn't?

The answer to each of those questions is the same: pride! The miserable one is filled with it; the other is not. The happy ones, in a sense, "lost to God" intentionally, surrendering all preconceived ideas, desires, and wants to the Lord, and therefore "won" the grace and help of God to enjoy whatever comes. The other prideful ones are still fighting to win their own wants and desires and preferences, a losing battle. Today's Bible verse is clear: "God resists the proud, but gives grace to the humble."

Which way this mission trip goes for you will depend on you. Life is 10% what happens to you, and 90% how you respond to it. Only you can choose your response. Will you lay down your pride, and lose your preferences to the Lord, or hold on to your desires and fight against Him?

Prayer: Lord I confess my need of You. I recognize that You rule over the affairs of this mission, and so I make a willful decision to embrace with thanksgiving the circumstance of the mission. I humble myself before Your mighty hand, and surrender all independence and right to "self rule." I don't want to find myself fighting against You, but cooperating with Your provision, schedule and plans for me.

DAY 24
SERVING THOSE IN CHARGE

1 Peter 5:5-6 *Likewise, you younger people, submit yourselves to your elders. Yes, all of you be submissive to one another, and be clothed with humility, for "God resists the proud, but gives grace to the humble." Therefore humble yourselves under the mighty hand of God, that he might exalt you in due time.*

Matthew 20:26 *whoever desires to become great among you, let him be your servant*

On your short-term mission, you might find yourself relating to a variety of Christian leaders: your team leader, national pastors, your hosts where you stay, ministry representatives, and long term missionaries. They are actually the perfect instruments God has fashioned for this time and place, a gift for you.

Leaders are amazing creatures! On one hand, they have qualities that cause you to open your heart to them and appreciate them. On the other hand, they sometimes make decisions that you might respond to with thoughts like "Why on earth are they asking me to do this?"

This trip will not be the opportune time to point out their shortcomings, or how they might do things differently, or how you would run the missionary program or the national church if you were in charge. That might sound silly; "I would never do that!" you respond. But on this mission, you will see things that you might think you would do differently "if you were them." Short-termers fall prey to this all too often and open their mouths pridefully in the intensity of the mission experience. It's one thing to offer a helpful, constructive idea to your team leader; it's quite another to have an attitude of superiority or to make suggestions to the national leadership when you do not have a long term relationship.

As a team member, serve your leaders and fellow team members with humility and embrace what the Lord wants to do in your life through them. Some of you might think of yourself as God's gift to your team, instead of realizing that they are God's gift to you.

The heart of a servant will always add strength to a leader and a team, and if you will make it your goal to do so, God will in return bless and honor you. God loves the attitude of a servant. You can really be a blessing to your team in many practical ways. See a need? Take initiative. Offer help. Look for how you can help get supplies and equipment ready or loaded before an outreach. Be ready to go here and there on time. Respond and follow directions quickly and eagerly, that leaders may lead and care for you with joy.

A servant's heart is a mark of maturity that is not dependent on a person's actual age, by the way. I've seen adult mission teams who were full of bad attitudes towards their leaders, and I've seen groups of 14 year olds who looked for every opportunity to take initiative and strengthen their leaders. Like all "good attitudes," this too is a choice, and one well worth making.

Prayer: Father, thank You again for the leaders You have chosen to bring across my path as gifts to me on this trip. I submit myself to You by submitting to those You've placed over me and around me. Fill my heart with a readiness to serve with humility and a readiness to receive the input You want to bring into my life through them.

DAY 25
THE DECEPTION THAT
RESULTS IN COMPLAINING

Philippians 2:14 *Do all things without complaining and disputing*

Proverbs 18:21 *Death and life are in the power of the tongue, And those who love it will eat its fruit.*

Romans 8:28 *And we know that all things work together for good to those who love God, to those who are the called according to His purpose.*

"Oh, that is the most disgusting, putrid smell" griped the man to me as he and his wife headed for the restaurant with us.

It was apparent that this man was not just slightly put off by the odor. Westerly breezes had perfectly funneled the smell of cow manure from nearby agricultural fields directly to our nostrils. He was really aggravated that his trip was being inconvenienced.

At first, I dismissed his remarks; after all, I never minded the smell of cow manure. Having grown up in rural NW Ohio, the smell of cow manure just stirs up some nostalgia for me (weird, I know).

As I walked with them towards the destination, I thought about the irony that this couple was about to enter a restaurant known for its incredible meatballs, which are made from cows. As we neared the door, the aroma of that great cooking sweetened the air. Then it hit me! You can't have these great smelling and tasting meatballs without ... COWS. And you can't have cows without ...MANURE! You could eliminate all cow manure smells from life, I suppose, but then, where would we get meatballs like that?

Certainly a mission trip can throw a lot of unexpected curves our way that are more intense and challenging than the smell of cow manure. And dealing with those challenges is more complicated than a self-help book on positive thinking.

Faith and praise are what you need to take with you. The enemy attempts to use every difficulty and inconvenience to deceive you into complaining. A complaint is really a statement that somehow God has failed you. Such statements influence people around you and weaken the group. That's why God hates complaining so much. Every inconvenience that comes your way will be an opportunity to grow, be changed, get stronger, and see God in a way you've never known Him before.

Complaining is a poor reflection of your own heart condition, it's an affront to God, and the sound of it is poison to others around you on the team.

Jehoshaphat greatly feared when told that a dangerous enemy army gathered to attack, but instead of whining and complaining, he sent singers out in front of his army to give thanks - BEFORE the battle. This act of faith (choosing to praise as a response to hardship) released the power of God to bring ultimate victory to God's people.

Whatever you'll face, or whatever kind of wind blows your way during this mission trip, keep your focus on the Lord, not on the wind. Be careful what you let roll off the end of your lips, and may it be thanks, not gripes. Because of your faith in God, you can trust that He's very much in control, and you should not be disappointed by temporary inconveniences.

Prayer: Father, I choose to approach this mission trip with praise on my lips, for You are a great God, and You are in charge. I thank You for all that You will have me encounter on this trip, both the pleasant and the unpleasant. I can thank You because I know that all things will work together for good for my teammates and me, because we love You and we are called according to Your purpose. Let my heart not embrace any temptation to complain, lest my complaints displease You, infect my team, or dull the effectiveness of this ministry.

DAY 26
I WILL GIVE YOUR ENEMY INTO YOUR HANDS

2 Corinthians 2:14 *Now thanks be to God who always leads us in triumph in Christ, and through us diffuses the fragrance of His knowledge in every place.*

Judges 4:6-7 *"The LORD, the God of Israel, commands you: 'Go, take with you ten thousand men of Naphtali and Zebulun and lead the way to Mount Tabor. I will lure Sisera, the commander of Jabin's army, with his chariots and his troops to the Kishon River and give him into your hands.'"*

I hosted a team which was traveling in a van to an extremely poor, drug-infested colonia on the edge of a large Mexican city, where they were going to be doing an outdoor evangelistic meeting. The city pastor who was planting a new church in this neighborhood was sharing information about the area as the group approached the destination.

"City buses won't go there because there is so much crime. Witches operate there, placing curses on people and keeping them in fear. Gangs rule and young girls who live in the colonia are never safe," Pastor Tony explained.

As we neared the site for the meeting, team members could see the blatant, demonic graffiti that covered some buildings.

The stories from Pastor Tony, now combined with these sights, caused a heavy silence to sink in on the mission team.

"Lord, give me wisdom" I whispered in prayer, wanting to know how to break off the fear and heaviness from the team. Immediately He showed me what was happening.

"Wait a minute!" I said excitedly. "This fear you are feeling is what the residents here live under all the time. Don't you see? The enemy has played his hand, and given you a taste of what the people are captive to. God does not intend for us to be intimidated here by this spirit of fear, but is letting you sense it so you can minister more effectively to the people. The spiritual forces at work here have revealed themselves, but we have not been captured by them. We are free of them! So we're going to *come in the opposite spirit.* Now that Satan's desire has been revealed, we are going to do the opposite, and come in bold courage."

That exhortation turned the tables; the team performed their music and drama and shared testimonies and preached with more boldness than ever. A few years later, that church plant has transformed the neighborhood. The buses are back; the gangs' influences are diminished; the colonia is a place of light where once darkness and fear reigned.

The incident gives us an example of what needs to be your battle strategy. Often you'll experience surprising struggles or emotions on a mission outreach that are not natural for you. Rather than accepting it as "your personal struggle," or even as your team's struggle, see it as the Lord showing you what spiritual strongholds the enemy has built up in the place where you are being sent. God's intent is to give the enemy of these souls into your hands. Then preach, testify, and come in the opposite spirit of that which you have been feeling, for the Spirit of God sent you there to weaken that thing on behalf of those He plans to set free.

Prayer: Lord, wherever we are sent, may we have the grace and ability to sense the spiritual strongholds, and may we have the perseverance to approach every moment of ministry in the power of the Holy Spirit. Use us to confront the powers of darkness, and bring a great victory for the church of Christ in that place. Thanks for giving our enemies into our hands, and we give You all the praise!

DAY 27
QUITTING IS NOT AN OPTION

Hebrews 10:35-39 "Therefore do not cast away your confidence, which has great reward. For you have need of endurance, so that after you have done the will of God, you may receive the promise:

> *'For yet a little while, And He who is coming will come and will not tarry. Now the just shall live by faith; But if anyone draws back, My soul has no pleasure in him.'*

But we are not of those who draw back to perdition, but of those who believe to the saving of the soul."

Who could imagine the many ways your life has been tested to this point? Surely there were surprises, and difficulties, and unexpectedly long trials that you have faced thus far. Maybe it was a long year with a difficult teacher at school. Maybe it's been a job that has just been monotonous and tedious; you've felt stuck there and not released by the Lord to go elsewhere. Or maybe it's been a long season of financial strain that often drained your strength.

And yet, here you are today by the grace of God, who brought you through those trials. You can look back on those difficulties as "past tense." Now you are on the brink of a mission trip to serve the Lord in some new environment. Surely this exciting opportunity will be nothing but thrills and happiness and one awesome experience after another! Right? Well, it might not be that simple.

As much as those past trials were not what you planned on, there are some new ones waiting for you that you have not even thought of yet. When they come, you'll be tested and tempted to look for a way of escape…an easier option. But as you surrender your fleshly desires for an easier way and lean on God, He'll sustain you and carry you to the fulfillment of every purpose He has for you in this mission. One day in the future, you'll look back on these trials as "past tense" also, if you don't quit.

Some of the most fruitful ministry I've ever been a part of has happened after some of the most difficult, tedious, and troubled travel. I've been on overnight trains and van rides packed with people, bus rides over mountains with people vomiting from all the switchbacks, rough commuter plane trips that turned my stomach, and bouncy trips through rough African grass-lands with surprises around every turn. And yet there at the end of every trail were some hungry souls for whom Jesus died, opening their hearts to the Truth and drawing out of us that which God had sent us to give.

The journey may be more difficult than you expected, but as you endure, the Lord works something in your life that is greatly pleasing to Him, and will one day result in a great reward.

<u>Prayer</u>: Lord, I thank You that You called me and that You are faithful to carry this mission to completion. Fulfill every purpose you have for me through this trip. As Your Word declares, I have need of endurance. As we are challenged during this mission, as our faith is stretched and the going gets difficult, and when I may even feel like giving up, I thank You that Your grace will be there for me. By that grace, I will be one You can take pleasure in, because I will not draw back or cast away my confidence in You.

DAY 28
EMBRACING A CULTURE AND
ITS BATHROOM

1 Corinthians 9:22 *I have become all things to all men, that I might by all means save some.*

1 Peter 2:17 *Honor all people.*

Philippians 2:3-4 *Let nothing be done through selfish ambition or conceit, but in lowliness of mind let each esteem others better than himself. Let each of you look out not only for his own interests, but also for the interests of others.*

A short-term mission trip is no time to influence a culture in any way other than by our message of the gospel.

Imagine your team traveling hours down bumpy roads, arriving at the remote village destination where you plan to minister. "Visitors! Here!" is the cry of the astonished residents. But after the long van ride, most of the mission team needs to find a bathroom before any ministry can happen. The villagers offer you their best bathroom, but for the next fifteen minutes they hear various ones from your team giggling to each other and saying "Eww!" while holding their noses at the unpleasant smell.

Now, ... do you think those villagers will want to hear your message? Sorry. An opportunity has been blown.

Laugh if you will, but it happens all the time, missionaries offending hosts over trivial differences in lifestyle, closing the door to effective ministry.

You can handle that bathroom! Toughen up! Keep your mouth closed!

Short-term inconveniences can be endured. God will sustain you with the food and shelter you need. You can go a short time without your favorite breakfast, junk foods, and snacks. If the host culture prefers it, you ladies can wear a skirt or dress if you need to, for an entire two weeks without complaint.

It's not a time to stretch the host country or host church's dress code by wearing clothes that they might find offensive, in the name of "freedom." It's not the time to express our desire for "some real food" or to discuss with the nationals "where WE live" or "at OUR church..." After all, it's not that your home church or culture is "better" than the one you are visiting; it's just "different."

Going back to the bathroom illustration, the fact is that even if the owners had more money, they probably wouldn't spend it on a new bathroom anyway. That's just not their priority. Are they wrong? Of course not; the culture is just different. Oh, and remember, YOU are the person that's different.

Smile through the unpleasant differences you notice, keeping your thoughts to yourself, and embrace the culture (which opens doors to the gospel), and enjoy the journey!

Prayer: Father, I acknowledge that You are the One who will care for me on this mission where much will be unfamiliar. You have placed qualities within this new culture which I go to embrace. Make me a pure and humble channel of Your truth and love. Give me eyes to see the treasure You have put in the host culture, that I might honor the people You send me to. By Your grace I will humble myself and look out for their needs rather than focus on my own.

DAY 29
PHOTO OPS AND
ETERNAL TREASURES

Luke 2:19 *But Mary treasured up all these things and pondered them in her heart.*

Romans 13:8 *Owe no one anything except to love one another, for he who loves another has fulfilled the law.*

Matthew 7:12 *So in everything, do to others what you would have them do to you, for this sums up the Law and the Prophets.*

I fought the urge to weep as I drove through a colonia in a large Mexican city to meet a national pastor. The abject poverty was unlike anything I had ever seen. The rest of our group was traveling in the vehicle ahead of me into the neighborhood. Alone in a small car following, I pondered the sights and choked back tears.

Then my own experience with the Lord was shattered by what happened next.

The vehicle in front stopped, an American short term missionary rolled down the van window, and stuck a big camera out towards a Mexican lady. She had just stepped out of her cardboard and tin shack in a worn, dirty dress to hang some clothing on a line.

I'm sure the photo would make a great news-letter piece for the missionary, but how did the woman feel? The woman's face appeared stunned at the site of these strangers driving by, gawking at her, and then ... *taking her picture*!

Did she have a nicer dress? We don't know. Was she proud of her property? I doubt it; she was obviously struggling just to live. Did the thought of some foreigners taking her picture excite her at the moment? Not in the least.

What would her response have been if, after the photo intrusion into her life of hardship, one of them had said, "By the way Señora, we're here to share with you about Jesus Christ." Their actions had already closed the door for any such possibility.

Obviously on a short term mission trip many team members are interested in some video footage or photos. Get as many as you can ... respectfully, and enjoy the memories later.

However, there are some experiences that you'll have and some things you're going to see that are going to be so astonishing, scenes that you are going to be itching to record by camera, which you need to "let go of." Out of love for the people God has sent you to, you are going to have to simply treasure the memories in your heart (or on paper) and keep them between you and the Lord.

In the Bible days, guess what? No cameras! Mary had no picture album to show her friends or with which to reminisce later about the star over Bethlehem, the shepherds, the magi, or the dedication of Jesus in the temple.

What did she do with these memorable, life changing, and historic events? The same thing that you are going to have to do... treasure them in your heart!

Prayer: Father, I thank You for the honor of going to new frontiers and for all of the new people and experiences and sights that You will bring my way. Help me to record as much as I can, whether through journals, photos, or videos. But Lord, I choose this day to treasure in my heart the memories of what You do, the places You take me, and what You bring my way. I choose this day to reject any selfish action that would be hurtful or hinder Your kingdom. Help me to walk in Your love at all times.

DAY 30
BARGAIN HUNTING AND
BARTERING, SOUVENIRS
AND SOULS

Luke 10:7 ... *the laborer is worthy of his wages*

2 Timothy 2:24 *And a servant of the Lord must not quarrel but be gentle to all*

"Hey, I bartered that blanket down to 140 pesos" the excited missionary yelled as he returned to the van. "Those sellers in the market may be slick, but I'm from the big city and they ain't going to get anything over on ME! You should have seen how frustrated that guy looked as I got him down to that price."

The team had enjoyed some much needed time off from ministry and had taken a trip down to a marketplace where they could get some souvenirs.

The ride back to base began with 20 minutes of loud bragging by team members, boasting over who had been most successful at sticking it to the "greedy marketplace workers" (I'm not making this up).

Gradually the conversation turned to speculation about what delicious dinner Elena the cook might have been preparing for us while we were away from base.

"What do you think those marketplace workers are having for dinner tonight?" I asked as I drove.

The question didn't sink in at first.

"Look, you saved yourself a couple of bucks, and will have a great meal to top off the day. Then in a few days you'll fly back home and be back in the office or school enjoying your future. Those workers will go home tonight, smear refried beans on some corn tortillas like they do every night, and be back at the market tomorrow and the next day. They'll stand on those concrete floors in their worn shoes for 12 hours every day, wondering if life will ever get any better. So now tell me, just WHAT did you win with your shrewd bargaining? What are they saying to each other about you right now, and what are they going to be thinking about you tonight when they lay down to rest?" (I know. I laid it on them pretty hard).

"Bartering" is expected in many countries. Typically, the seller sees the well-to-do visitors and starts the process with a price much higher than he's actually willing to accept.

We were advised by national workers never to pay the initial asking price. None of us wants to be taken advantage of by seasoned and some-times unscrupulous sellers. But since when is the marketplace a battlefield? Our goal is not to "defeat" or "conquer" the seller, nor should we find any personal satisfaction in leaving a seller frustrated. If you find what you want for a good price, buy it. If it costs too much, go on.

Personally, I've found that if you just wait a moment to translate and process their initial asking price in your head, they'll come down at least once and often twice even before you say anything (by that time I know the seller is starting to get reasonable).

Comparing the prices at a couple of other stands also helps judge what's an appropriate price.

A trip to the market is not "time off" from being a representative of Christ and a carrier of His presence. Our true enemies are spiritual, and the inheritance we seek and have been praying for is the eternal salvation of souls, not a bag full of cheap trinkets.

Prayer: Oh God, I desire to be a warrior in the real battles You send me to and not get caught up in strife for any reason. Let me not be contentious with mankind for the sake of my own personal gain. You are a God of patience and goodness. It is Your kindness that leads men to repentance. Let that fruit of the Spirit increase in my heart and mind and flow from my life daily.

SPECIAL DAY OF PRAYER AND FASTING FOR YOUR MINISTRY

Isaiah 58:6 *Is this not the fast that I have chosen: To loose the bonds of wickedness,*
To undo the heavy burdens, To let the oppressed go free, And that you break every yoke?

1 Corinthians 15:58 *Beloved brethren, be steadfast, immovable, always abounding in the work of the Lord, knowing that your labor is not in vain in the Lord.*

Today, take some extra time to pray more specifically for your short term mission ministry. Consider again how the Lord would have you fast (all day, one meal). Your team's ministry plan is either being formed, or has already been laid out with some level of detail. However, there are sure to be surprises in store, and even within the existing plan, there are many specifics which are impossible for you to anticipate. Ask the Lord to direct your steps and the steps and thinking of the leaders who will be making decisions. Take some time to lift those things before the Lord. Ask Him for signs and wonders to follow your outreach, and for a fruitful ministry. Ask Him to prepare your heart for what is to come. Ask Him for success in all that you set your hands to do.

Look back over the devotionals you've read so far, and see if the Lord would want you to review one again and focus more prayer about a particular day's devotional.

Today, as you get closer to the time of the mission trip, spend some time offering prayers, thanks, and praises to God. Are there specific issues or practical prayer needs that your team has discussed which you can spend some focused time today praying about? Or are there particular issues that you have been uneasy about? Right now, lift those concerns to the Lord and let Him carry them for you, and let's see what He will do! Watch Him move in behalf of the mission.

_____ Team leader

_____ Location we are headed

Primary type of work for this team (evangelism, construction, intercessory prayer, leadership training,children'sministry,literaturedistribution, church ministry, other): _____

_____

Ministry plans as we know them so far: _____

_____

_____

Issues of concern the team has discussed: _____

_____

_____

Issues I have been uneasy or worried about: ____

_____

_____

DAY 31
EMBRACING A CULTURE:
MANGY DOGS AND LITTER

Psalm 141:3 *Set a guard, O LORD, over my mouth; Keep watch over the door of my lips.*

1 Corinthians 10:31-33 *Therefore, whether you eat or drink, or whatever you do, do all to the glory of God. Give no offense, either to the Jews or to the Greeks or to the church of God, just as I also please all men in all things, not seeking my own profit, but the profit of many, that they may be saved.*

It was only my third mission trip, and the first for many years. I couldn't help but notice how "different" so many things were in this new country. Riding with a pastor friend from the U.S., who then picked up a young interpreter from the city, we drove along rather quietly, until yet another large, thin dog with ribs showing crossed the street in front of us.

"Man, the dogs here are sure mangy-looking, aren't they?" I observed.

Now, my observation was correct, and so the comment might have seemed warranted. But out of the corner of my eye, I saw the interpreter visibly recoil with disgust, and my pastor friend quickly changed the subject.

What had I done wrong? Why the offense?

I had mistakenly equated "different" with "not as good."

In that host country, dogs are for protection, not for pets, and most need to find food on their own. There, people are struggling to feed their children; they would consider it a waste to spend their limited resources on a dog's health. In my country, every dog is a beloved part of the family, with careful and expensive treatment; most masters spend more on their dogs than they give to the poor. Which perspective is *better*? The truth is, you could argue about which is more *moral*; but each perspective is simply *different*.

Another time I was in a van full of short-termers when a team member asked the interpreter "Why is there so much trash everywhere? You can't litter where we're from. Don't people here care about litter?"

(After contemplating murder) I used it as a teaching moment to explain the context of the national people's basic need to survive outweighing the opportunity to give any priority to picking up roadsides.

It's tempting when you meet someone who speaks your language, to let your guard down and begin asking them the questions that come to your mind about the "different things" you've noticed.

Be VERY careful in those moments. Offending someone is not worth the small exchange of information.

And remember that "different" does not mean "better" ... or "worse."

Prayer: Lord I confess my need of Your help in setting watch over the door of my lips. In any careless moment, I pray that You will look to this altar of prayer and answer me then in that moment of conversation. Help me not to speak of my observations in any way that would hurt a person in the land that You send me to. I endeavor, by Your grace, to consider other people more important than me, their thoughts more important than mine, their lives more important than mine, every moment I'm there. I choose with Your help to embrace the culture You send me to, with no concern for incidental differences, but only a heart to love them and declare only the words You give me.

DAY 32
LORD, HOW COULD I
EVER DOUBT YOU?

Mark 4:35-41 *On the same day, when evening had come, He said to them, "Let us cross over to the other side." ... And a great windstorm arose, and the waves beat into the boat, so that it was already filling. But He was in the stern, asleep on a pillow. And they awoke Him and said to Him, "Teacher, do You not care that we are perishing?"*

Then He arose and rebuked the wind, and said to the sea, "Peace, be still!" And the wind ceased and there was a great calm. But He said to them, "Why are you so fearful? How is it that you have no faith?" And they feared exceedingly, and said to one another, "Who can this be, that even the wind and the sea obey Him!"

2 Corinthians 4:17 *For our light affliction, which is but for a moment, is working for us a far more exceeding and eternal weight of glory*

Matthew 28:20 *"and lo, I am with you always, even to the end of the age."*

We were a young couple on our first short term mission, flying half way across the country with an infant, joining a Youth With a Mission outreach to Asian refugees in inner city Denver. We were going with our local church's blessing, and with great encouragement that the Lord was with us. But within a few hours of landing, our belongings were sitting in a pile on a gym floor along with those of 75 other people. Realizing that we might be sleeping on the floor along with a whole bunch of other people, my wife and I experienced a strong temptation to panic.

"We can't sleep on a school floor for a week with a baby!"

We were certain that the mission staff hadn't thought the arrangements through at all, that we had made a tragic mistake in coming, and that this would be a disastrous week. In reality, God worked it all out, and it turned into an incredible week of experiences that changed our lives.

Jesus once said "Let's cross over to the other side." The disciples obeyed, with Jesus along in the boat. Then a wind rocked the boat and the 12 "men of faith and power" panicked. They were filled with doubt over two thoughts that they entertained:

1) "Lord, don't you care?" – When God has the power to do something about the difficult circumstances you are facing,

will you trust Him? When He can make it all better, and the going is still tough, will you doubt His concern for you? It's the core truth that Satan wants to undermine in your mind: the fact that God loves you.

2) "We are perishing!" – When it begins to feel like the ship is going down, or you are not going to make it, it's easy to hit the panic button.

You are on this mission trip, with the King of the Universe alongside, just as He promised. He is not afraid of trouble along the way. While God has a ministry purpose for your going on this mission, He is also interested in "conforming you to His image" along the way. He will continue to do so even when circumstances threaten to strike fear in your emotions. If you should find yourself encountering conditions that seem like they are going to make your trip a disaster, remember that God intends for an awesome experience. Don't panic, disciple of faith and power! Trust Him. He's still in the boat, He cares, and you are not perishing.

Prayer: Lord, You desire to work through me, as well as in me, during this mission trip. For every detail of the trip that has already been planned out, there are still unexpected experiences awaiting, some that might seem to threaten harm. So even now, when all is calm, I pray about the times on this mission when things are not so calm. I thank You that You will be with me, and that the circumstances are submitted to Your kingdom purposes. Lead us past each obstacle, I pray, with our eyes open to Your great power, that we may not be overcome by fear, but rather that we might continue in obedience, faith and love.

DAY 33
A POWERFUL PIECE
OF YOUR ARMOR

1 Peter 4:1 *Therefore, since Christ suffered in His body, <u>arm</u> <u>yourself</u> also with this mindset.*

2 Timothy 2:3 *Endure hardship with us, like a good soldier of Christ Jesus.*

The group had left their home before dawn to meet at church and travel to the airport. The long flight to their new mission field was followed by a two hour van ride to the facility made ready for them. They had prayed many hours together and prepared creative and dynamic evangelistic ministry with a desire to bring many souls to Christ.

"This place has only five bathrooms for 34 people?" came the first complaint when they arrived at the base where I hosted. Then it was the food: "I'm not eating this slop all week!" one member declared (I wasn't cooking, but I still didn't appreciate it).

"Bunk beds? I've never slept in bunk beds before. I can't believe this!"

One brother came to me aside, "Where can I rent a car in this country so I can have some freedom? I can't take these people on this team."

(Actually, I almost couldn't take them either by this time, but for different reasons).

Needless to say, the team leader and I had our hands full. In fact, I almost packed them all back on the plane and sent them home, the onslaught of griping was so bad.

What happened? This team, so versed in spiritual warfare, knew about the "sword of the Spirit" and "the shield of faith" and the power of prayer and the blood of Jesus Christ. But in all of their preparation, they had left one Biblical piece of their armor at home, and their ministry effectiveness was diminished because of it.

What is that piece of armor? "<u>The mind to suffer hardship</u>!"

This team could have told you all the "weapons of our warfare" that are commonly quoted as part of the armor of God, but they were missing "the mind to suffer hardships" that the Bible speaks of in First Peter.

What an amazing level of vulnerability is snuffed out when each team member makes a decision both to enjoy God's blessings, and to endure whatever difficult circumstances may arise. Arming yourself with a willingness to experience hardship will deflect the fiery, tempting dart of complaining, lift your spirits above inconveniences, and bring you into a victorious level of ministry.

When packing your bags, don't forget to pack "a mind to suffer hardship" like a good soldier.

Prayer: Father, grant me spiritual eyes to see Your goodness throughout the mission, despite whatever logistical difficulties or obstacles may come my way. I arm myself with that mindset, knowing that life during this mission will not be what I'm accustomed to. I submit myself to You and make a decision of my will, right now, to undergo hardship as one of Your good soldiers.

DAY 34
WATER INTO WINE AND
GUNK INTO WATER

Mark 10:27 *But Jesus looked at them and said, "With men it is impossible, but not with God; for with God all things are possible."*

Mark 16:20 *And they went out and preached everywhere, the Lord working with them and confirming the word through the accompanying signs.*

Many of these devotionals have perhaps sounded like warnings to expect difficulty, and you certainly should go on your short term mission trip ready to endure hardships. That IS an important part of your mental armor.

However, you should also go in the confidence that you have been sent by a great God, a miracle working God, a powerful God, One who has promised to go with you.

I took one group abroad to help build a church building, and they had endured tremendous physical hardships, but had kept a victorious attitude during their mission. They had encouraged one another through sickness, tough climate and work conditions, and many other difficult challenges.

Water had been in short supply for the needs of cement mixing, but neighbors in the community where the church was being built had donated as much of their precious water as they could to the host pastor for the project.

As the project was nearing completion and the team's time there was nearly over, they ran out of all water, except for a sewer-like, smelly, green, grungy cistern of water at a nearby abandoned property. Who knows what sicknesses and diseases and critters were thriving in that water! We passed by it several times a day, but the pastor and the team had been avoiding this water all week. On the project's last day, with reluctance, the gracious host pastor informed the team that they were going to have to begin carrying buckets of THAT water to the work site, in order to finish the job.

Two workers in charge of "the water bucket brigade," as they called themselves, knelt together and prayed, saying "Lord, we didn't come here with our own agenda. We've been willing to do anything You asked of us, and we are still willing. You know our hearts; we don't WANT to get anywhere near that water, much less carry it here and use it in the cement, but we will, because You have sent us to do so. We ask that You protect us and our teammates from sickness and bacteria, as we continue to do Your will, in Jesus' name. Amen."

To their shock, when they got to the stagnant cistern with their buckets, that same water which had been putrid only a few hours before, was as fresh as a mountain stream! No smell, no green, no grunge, and no fear! They had experienced a miracle. What a celebration of praise and thanks we had as we finished the mission!

When you need one, there's a miracle there for you too.

Prayer: Lord, forgive me if I have made You too small in my sight. Thank You for going with us on this mission trip. You are a great God, and You do miracles. Thanks for meeting all of our needs, for the grace to endure hardship, and for rescuing us when we need a miracle. We love You, and trust You, and are glad that we serve a Big God.

DAY 35
WHY DOES THIS FEEL SO WEIRD?

John 1:12 *But as many as received Him, to them He gave the right to become children of God, to those who believe in His name*

"This is not my usual schedule. I'm not getting up like I usually do in the usual manner. I don't have to go to work today at my usual place of employment. My schedule is being determined by other people. And everywhere I go, I'm with these other people I call 'teammates.' I can't get away from them. I don't have the independence I'm used to. I can't jump in the car and go where I want, when I want. Others are telling me what I'll eat, where I'll sleep, when I'll shower, and what I'll do most of the day."

Ah, the life of a short term missionary! Glamorous. Adventurous. Exciting. And, ... trying! It's normal for a short term missionary to experience some emotional shock at the feeling of "not controlling" your life. We may *say* that God has always been in control of our life but on a short term mission we *feel* more "out of control," as our independence gets swallowed up in team ministry.

If individuals continue to hold on to and exercise their personal "rights" to be an independent person ("my schedule, my privacy and personal space, my freedom"), living their own agenda, they'll miss God's best for the team. Whether it's a mission team, sports team, or family, they and the team will miss God's best.

In many countries, we are so accustomed to fighting for "our political rights." The only "right" the Bible speaks about Christians having, however, is "the right to become children of God."

The interesting thing about being a child is that, in a family, children can be told what to do and they can be disciplined. So, having "the right to become a child of God" means we may need to be told things that would not occur to our mind otherwise. You are going to be told some things to do on your short term mission trip. You will be given a schedule not of your own making and you may not choose your roommate or sleep schedule. We are so accustomed to "our freedoms" that it may feel weird. Be assured that you're NOT going crazy, those feelings are normal, and you will be just fine, ... IF you let go of that independent will of yours!

Prayer: Lord I surrender to You all of the personal rights I have embraced, "losing" them for the cause of this team and Your gospel. Grant me grace to remain in that place of surrender, when the reality of my lost independence tests my patience, feelings, love, and faith.

DAY 36
THE TESTING OF FRIENDSHIPS

Proverbs 10:12 *"Love covers a multitude of sins"*

Matthew 18:15 *Moreover if your brother sins against you, go and tell him his fault between you and him alone. If he hears you, you have gained your brother.*

Your humility and patience will be tested on this mission, most intensely by the day-in, day-out presence of your teammates (some of whom may be your closest friends or even family).

The most common testing is just the little things in each of us that "bug" one another. The quirks of your teammates will bug you, and yours will bug them (yes, that's true). Don't let walls divide, but purpose in your heart to love.

Feeling awkward around a particular team member?

Ask yourself this question: "Is this just me being irritated by a personality, or have I really been hurt by something they said or did?"

If it's just a matter of personality, then the responsibility rests on you and the key will be to come before God in brokenness. Daily devotional times with Him are essential to get in touch with him, to draw from His grace and to receive

His love. Ask Him to disconnect the "buttons" that Satan likes to push in you. Repent of all selfish thinking, embrace God's love for you and your teammates, and pray for your fellow team members as gifts from the Lord. Ask Him to show you ways that you can demonstrate His love by living your life for the benefit of others, including your teammates.

Realize that every problem is not always just a personality clash, however. Sometimes, a person will actually hurt or sin against you. For the sake of yourself and the team don't let these things "simmer" inside you for days on end, allowing unforgiveness or some bad attitude to prevail in your thinking. Get alone with the person and say, "You know, when you said '…,' I felt put down or hurt. Is that what you meant to do?"

This is the first step in Jesus' instructions of Matthew 18, and usually, conversations like this are all it takes to restore unity. Most people don't wake up in the morning and decide, "Today, I'm going go out and hurt that person." Usually, Christians will welcome being told if something they did offended or hurt you, and appreciate the opportunity to express their heart. When they respond in sorrow, you respond with forgiveness. If the person is hardened towards you, then bring in the team leader for perspective and resolution; don't let the team spirit be harmed or the group be divided.

Prayer: Lord, thank You for the opportunity to grow in love and patience while being used by You in the mission field. Let me have Your perspective and unconditional love for my teammates, as You Father, also love us unconditionally. You have chosen us together for such a time as this. May we please You by all that we do, and in all that we say and think, as we walk together in unity.

DAY 37
WALK IN THE LIGHT

1 John 1:7 *But if we walk in the light as He is in the light, we have fellowship with one another, and the blood of Jesus Christ His Son cleanses us from all sin.*

Mark 2:5 *When Jesus saw their faith, He said to the paralytic, "Son, your sins are forgiven you."*

A young man on our Colombia mission team had been grappling with faraway thoughts for a couple of days. He wasn't himself. Something was wrong, but we didn't have any way of knowing what it was.

Finally, he came to some other brothers in the mission group and said, "Do you remember a couple nights ago in Bogota, when our whole team was walking several blocks to the church for the evening service, and that prostitute called out for us guys from the street corner?"

Then, he confided, "I feel silly having to even say this, but ever since then, I've been bombarded with impure thoughts. I don't know what it is. I've tried praying and asking God to help me with this whole thought pattern, but I can't seem to shake it. I can't stop my mind from continuously wandering down a wrong road. Would you please pray for me?"

The brothers gathered around him without any sense of judgment, prayed for him, and this pattern of thinking was broken easily.

Why could the young man be free after taking this step, when he couldn't get free on his own? Because God resists the proud, gives grace to the humble, and does not intend for any of us to succeed alone.

The team members in this case served just like the friends of the paralytic who, in one of the gospel stories, carried the lame man to Jesus and let him down through the roof. The Bible says that Jesus saw *their* faith and healed the paralytic. It doesn't say the paralytic could do anything for himself.

We all have some area of life where we can become paralyzed, needing another's help on occasion.

Are you struggling with a pattern of thinking, be it impurity, anger, depression, despair, or some other manifestations of darkness? Have you tried to break out of it but couldn't?

There isn't time on a short term mission to let days go by in this state and ruin your trip. Ask a trusted confidant to pray with you. God's cleansing grace and a victorious breakthrough await you when you bring it to the light of a trusted friend.

Prayer: Father, You have chosen me together with each team member, because we need one another. I humble myself before You and them, opening my heart and praying that in me there should be no hidden area of darkness, no foothold for the enemy to take. Help us strengthen one another and to carry each other to You in prayer.

DAY 38
IS THIS WORTH ALL THE
MONEY TO GO?

2 Corinthians 4:5-7 *...we do not preach ourselves, but Christ Jesus the Lord, and ourselves your bondservants for Jesus' sake. For it is the God who commanded light to shine out of darkness, who has shone in our hearts to give the light of the knowledge of the glory of God in the face of Jesus Christ. But we have this treasure in earthen vessels, that the excellence of the power may be of God and not of us.*

The thought may come to your mind that this short term mission trip is an awful lot of money. In fact, there is one school of thought out there in Christian circles that says wealthy nations should send their money, and NOT people, on short term mission trips. "After all," the logic declares, "the nationals can do so much more with that amount of money than you can."

There is one major problem with that "logical" view. Nowhere in the Bible does it say that God inhabits money! God dwells in people! He has said "Go," He is sending you, and has promised to go with you. God has placed something in you that can never dwell in a currency, and that is a deposit of Himself.

The reason that Jesus said "Go" is because one person has the strength from God that another person needs. We in this country need the strength that God has deposited in Christians from other parts of the world, and vice versa.

You are being sent to places where you are going to pray, preach, sing, testify, build, or train leaders like only you can do. No dollar bill can do it. You are going to meet people and form relationships that no amount of money can accomplish.

Does God have the necessary resources to see His own commands fulfilled or not?

Economic markets rise and fall, but God has no shortage of dollar bills, pesos, pounds, schillings, and other currencies. The Bible says that the earth is His and the fullness thereof. In other words: it all belongs to Him. His bank account is unlimited, although He does sometimes have a shortage of obedient servants who will go into all the world.

The Lord spoke to me to train pastors on short term missions in two impoverished nations. My logical mind thought "They can't afford it," but I obeyed and challenged them to begin doing what they *could* afford, like sending teams across the city or to neighboring villages. As they did what they could do, I assured them that God would open more doors.

I myself was shocked only a few years later, when I found some of these pastors bringing teams to *my* country on short term mission trips! One pastor came up to me and said "I remember you! You taught us about going, and we're doing what you taught us."

Don't let the logic of human reasoning over-step the clear command of Scripture, and get going with joy!

Prayer: Lord, You have shone Your light into my life and You are taking me to places where that light can shine, dispelling all darkness. Let my life always be a carrier of Your light, for You are the treasure that lives in me. During this short term mission, may there be an exchange between cultures that brings life both to mine, and to the culture You send us to.

DAY 39
LEAVING STUFF BEHIND

Proverbs 3:5-7 *Trust in the LORD with all your heart, And lean not on your own understanding; In all your ways acknowledge Him, And He shall direct your paths. Do not be wise in your own eyes; Fear the LORD and depart from evil.*

James 1:5 *If any of you lacks wisdom, let him ask of God, who gives to all liberally and without reproach*

As you near the time of returning home, a practical issue you'll deal with is the desire to leave things behind. Depending on the culture you go to and the needs you observe, you may be deeply moved to want to leave clothing, etc. behind.

In Cuba, the needs were so overwhelming that our hosts even pleaded with us that we might let them keep our empty drinking water bottles, and the plastic grocery bags that we had used to bring some supplies in.

Today's devotional is not intended to curb your God-given generosity at all. In fact, be a blessing in every way you can! I do want to caution you to make sure you listen carefully to the Lord, however, being aware that the manner in which you give can affect whole groups of people. I know of cultures where the gift of one wrist watch can send a message that would leave some grappling with offense issues for a long time.

Excessive fanfare while giving something to one person in front of others can also elicit a jealousy from the others that may linger long after you're gone. In many cases where the culture is hard pressed by severe economic hardships, gifts left behind inappropriately can motivate people to see future mission teams as opportunities for personal gain.

Certainly if you love the Lord and He's at work in your heart, then you are a generous person who will want to help when observing genuine need. National Christians may have served you and helped make your mission experience awesome. You'd like to reward them for their faithfulness. God may knit your heart to some very likable people, and it's very tempting to pick out certain "favorites" to whom you want to give something, but again, you have to be careful of offense.

In general, one way to handle this is to leave your gift with a host Pastor with integrity, or host missionary, or another leader of honesty. They are the ones who have had a longer time to know the people intimately, and who have perspective on true need. That person will be dealing with the aftermath there long after you are gone and will make distribution decisions based on the long term health of the national church. Your giving will be channeled through a leader who is better suited to deliver it in a way that is consistent with the Lord's vision for that ministry.

Admittedly, by doing this you lose control of how your goods are distributed. This is why it takes trust to give and yet leave the distribution to the Lord. You can trust the Lord to let the man or woman in charge carry the responsibility for wise distribution.

If you have money or a gift in particular you want to give a special person you've met, then I would recommend at least expressing that desire to the national pastor, host missionary, or leader of integrity. Make sure they don't have a reason for you not to do so. They'll appreciate your checking with them, and may have suggestions that will prevent a problem down the road.

Prayer: Father, I am open to being used by You in any way You lead me, including sharing the bounty You've given me with others who have less than I do. All I have is Yours and not my own, so do with it as You want. I acknowledge that my unfamiliarity with the personal dynamics in this new land may make me vulnerable to misconceptions that could cause problems, so I ask for Your wisdom and for grace in giving. Protect the people You send us to. I

gladly submit my preferences to You and to
the long term leadership You've planted there.
In anything I share, be it spiritual, practical, or
material, let it all give honor to You and may it
advance Your purposes.

DAY 40
REENTRY INTO THE ATMOSPHERE

Luke 10:17-20 *Then the seventy returned with joy, saying, "Lord, even the demons are subject to us in Your name." And He said to them, "I saw Satan fall like lightning from heaven. Behold, I give you the authority to trample on serpents and scorpions, and over all the power of the enemy, and nothing shall by any means hurt you. Nevertheless do not rejoice in this, that the spirits are subject to you, but rather rejoice because your names are written in heaven."*

When space agencies send a rocket into space, they don't wait until the ship is about to come home to begin planning for the reentry. Planning for reentry is in fact one of the most critical aspects of space exploration. Incredible energy, research, engineering, and thought go into that dangerous passage from outer space back into the atmosphere of earth. Without careful planning for reentry, the shuttle or spaceship would disintegrate and the benefits of the exploratory mission would be lost in the tragedy.

Likewise, the benefits of your mission can be lost without planning for "reentry" into your home culture. Preparation for a short term mission is not just about the going, but also about the returning.

You will have many experiences that will deeply affect you. You won't be able to process it all immediately, but you will be returning with a new set of "spiritual eyes." Business as usual may not come easy for you.

Missionaries can sometimes struggle with various emotions that they weren't expecting upon return: grief and sadness, loss of motivation for the old routines of work, or reverse culture shock. One short-termer we brought back from Cuba expressed tremendous anger and disdain for our own culture and Western prosperity. Some have come back with a "chip on their shoulder" of spiritual pride (castigating their brothers and sisters that didn't go).

You can help yourself with these adjustments, bring closure at the end of your mission, and maximize the benefit to your life and those you touch by doing several things. First, keeping a journal of your mission will be valuable to you later, helping you benefit from the experiences even after you are back. Secondly, before leaving the places of your ministry to come home, take time to say quality "good byes" to those who made your experience significant. Leaving can be difficult, but this will help avoid the feeling that there are a lot of emotional "loose ends" hanging out there, untied. Saying quality good byes also seems to help us emotionally prepare to reconnect with loved ones back home. Finally, spend some time with teammates before leaving, "debriefing." Discuss together your perceptions of the mission, how God worked in you and through you, what you are thankful for, what you are looking forward to, and what the return home means for each of you.

The disciples of Jesus returned ecstatic about their mission. Jesus reminded them to preserve a humble mindset, being thankful foremost, that God had saved them to eternal life.

Prayer: Lord, prepare us for the journey there and for the journey home. Help us extract as much of the benefits of this experience as possible. Keep us ever mindful that our lives are not our own, whether abroad or at home, and that our deepest joy and thanks is due You just because You died for us to save us from our sins. Any way that You use us beyond this is just an extra blessing, and even for that, we will be careful to give You the glory.

ABOUT THE AUTHOR

Jack Hempfling has served since March of 2001 as the Senior Pastor of Living Waters Church, in LeRoy, NY. He has previously authored two leadership articles for Ministry Today magazine.

His unlikely launch into missions began in 1985. As a young married couple with a small child, Jack and his wife, Sandy, left their home in Columbus, Ohio to attend a one-week outreach at Youth With a Mission's new base in Denver, Colorado. Soon after, they joined a Discipleship Training School. Just before leaving to go to the DTS, one of the staff pastors at The Redeemer's Church in Columbus said during a time of prayer for the Hempflings, "I have a sense that while on this mission trip and training school, the Lord is going to give you a key that will open up a great door of service to the Body of Christ in the future."

While at YWAM, the Lord imparted to Jack a vision for seeing para-church and church-based short term mission teams equipped and sent to impact the nations, and for seeing a heart for the nations woven throughout the fabric of local churches.

Since then, he has served in both local church pastoral ministry and as the Short Term Mission Director for Harvest Preparation International Ministries (HPIM). Both his pastor's heart and his loyalty to the Great Commission will leap off the pages of this devotional.

Over the years, Jack has been a part of numerous short term mission teams, and, while at HPIM, has led and facilitated hundreds of short term missionaries from the U.S. to the world. God has also used him to challenge local church leaders in other nations to become nations-conscious churches and to be part of what the Lord is doing in short term missions in these days. There are now international churches involved in sending teams from the developing world that owe their missions sending vision to Jack's exhortation.

Jack has traveled extensively in many parts of Mexico, as well as to Colombia, Haiti, Cuba, Uganda and Kenya with either short term mission teams or leadership training seminars.

The stories, illustrations, and quips you read in this devotional are not theological principles made up in a class room, but are born out of Jack's personal real-life experiences and associations with short term mission groups. It's his fervent hope that you are blessed in your time with the Lord Jesus Christ while using this devotional tool.

CPSIA information can be obtained at www.ICGtesting.com
Printed in the USA
BVOW02s0631300316

442282BV00001B/16/P